Mantras, Meditations, & Math

Mantras, Meditations, & Math

MEL DUNNUCK

ISBN-978-1-7379490-0-8

CONTENTS

PLANTS

I believe in treating people like plants. I believe in treating myself like a plant. More specifically, I believe in treating relationships like house plants. This means that when a relationship is struggling, you do not simply give up. You would not just throw away a plant if it starts turning colors. When this happens, you either change the environment in which it grows, or give the plant more attention. A plant can be given more attention by watering the plant with a different amount of water or on less or more days, changing the amount of sunlight it is getting, or putting it in a different pot. You do not just throw away the plant.

Treat all relationships like this. Most importantly, treat your relationship with yourself like this. Treat yourself like a plant, and everything will change. I mean by this that you should drink enough water, nurture yourself properly with fruits and vegetables, spend time in the sunlight, and do things that make your soul happy. Talk nicely to yourself and practice positivity and gratitude. That is how you can treat yourself like a plant.

Plants are a gift to us from the Earth. Plants give us food, oxygen, homes, clothes, and medicine. When we have plants in our homes, they help clarify the air and they help clear our minds. It is good to have plants in the house. Growing plants can be therapeutic. When we grow plants, we have something to take care of that is not just ourselves. We must respond to the plant's needs and realize when we need to change the amount of water or sunlight that the plant is getting.

I think plants can teach us lots of lessons, too. There is so much to be learned from the trees. They teach us to stand tall, to use the riches that the Earth offers, and to be strong. Trees teach us to grow and expand, which brings me to the tree theory. The tree theory is something I made while looking at the beautiful and majestic oak trees on St. Charles Avenue in New Orleans. Trees have lots of roots, just like people and ideas do. After the root comes the tree trunk. The tree trunk grows and expands as the tree grows taller, older, and wiser. The trunk or base of an idea or a human increasingly grows over time. The top of the tree has the branches, and the number of branches that a tree has is not a set number. Trees have varying numbers of branches, and the branches differ in size, too. Trees all look a little different, just like people do. The tree theory explains the similarities of trees to human beings and ideas.

Just like people, trees can benefit from being surrounded by other trees. Some groups of trees synchronize their rate of photosynthesis and their use of nutrients, ensuring that there will be enough resources for all the trees in the community. Imagine if people worked this way. We can surround ourselves with each other to learn and grow. We can also surround our ideas with more ideas to strengthen and enrich them. We need each other.

Trees are like people and ideas because they all grow. They all start from something small and grow into something much greater. The large oak trees on St. Charles Avenue did not become what they are overnight. In fact, it took them years to become what they are today. People and ideas are the same way. They both need to develop to become something greater than what they already are. A seed might be destined to be a great tree, but it must grow to be healthy, to be strong, and to hold its own. People and ideas are the same way.

There are times when we truly connect with people. There are times that we experience rapport with others, and there are times when we feel harmonious relationships. We feel human-to-human connection, and we feel real human-to-human love. We can see the light within others when we feel this. We also have a connection to plants. The trees help us breathe. When we see a beautiful flower, it can put a smile on our faces. We are connected with plants and people.

Plants teach us not to give up. When a plant starts to turn colors or die, it can come back to life. It can come back with some extra love and care. When a plant changes colors, it might need more sunlight. It also could need less. It might need to be put in a pot that fits its size better, or it might need to be watered more. It seems strange, but the plant might be getting too much water and it might need to be watered less. Whatever the issue is, the plant just needs something different. It does not need you to give up on it, it just needs change.

Like plants, people struggle at times, too. You might need to give them more space or more love for them to grow properly. People feel the most love when you give them time and an open and listening ear. We must not forget that when a plant is struggling, you change the environment in which it grows. We need to remember this because it applies to people, too.

Going back to the tree theory, I think that we can all learn from our roots. We can learn from trees that we need our roots to survive. We can get to the roots of issues, the roots of ideas, and to the roots of people. Every problem in your life has a root. We need to get to the roots. Human beings have roots. We have the places where we are from, the places we feel comfortable in, and the people we feel comfortable with. We have stories and we have events and times that have passed. In our roots, we also find that we reflect others. We reflect the people that we love, the people that we meet, and the people who raised us. I believe that I am a reflection of powerful women in my life, including my mother, aunts, and my Granny.

Trees lose their leaves every year and they still come back because of everything around them. We are very connected to each other as humans, and as humans who share this ground with all the plants and animals on it, we are connected to them as well. The ground connects us all. All living things are living together on this earth at the same time. The roots of a tree are connected to the ground. We are all standing on the ground, just like the trees. We have roots too; we just cannot see them with our eyes. We know that we have roots because we can feel them inside of us. We have places and people that feel like home, and these are our roots.

We can get to our own roots. We can try to understand which people have influenced us and in which ways they have done so. We can think about the people who have inspired us the most in our lives. We can think about our own stories and we can think about why we have done the things we have done, and why we do the things that we are doing. It is important to ask ourselves why we do the things that we do. These are our roots.

For as long as I can remember, most of the females on my mom's side of the family have been plant people. I mean they are plant people because not only do they grow many plants as food, but they also have many plants around the house as decoration. Like me, they just love plants. Their daughters also love plants. One of my cousins has at least 50 plants in her bay window. For my birthday this past year, I received plants from my aunts. My Granny has a spectacular garden. I believe there is a correlation between being a good mother and being good at taking care of plants. I also believe there is something special about people who like to take care of plants. I know there is something special about those who treat people like plants.

One of my Granny's mantras is that you do not have to be friends with everyone, but you should be friendly to everyone. I remember my Granny saying this mantra when I was younger and I remember my mom telling it to me, too. Granny told me that this mantra was one of the things she wanted to teach her kids when they were growing up. She wanted to teach her kids about respect. It was also very important to her that they learned about kindness and love. She told me she was always instructing them to try to get along. She taught them not to make fun of others and that if you see someone who needs help, you should help them.

I asked my mom what she learned from Granny, and she told me the same mantra that Granny told me about being friendly to everyone. She also learned that there is always more love. There is room for more love of people, animals, plants, books, music, and experiences. Granny had eight kids and has many grandchildren and even a few great-grandchildren. From this, she knows that love is not limited.

I asked my Granny about her garden. I asked her why she likes to have one, and she told me that she loves her garden because it is therapeutic and peaceful. When she is in it, she forgets about the outside world. She thinks about what a wonder it is that God can take a seed and turn it into a plant. That plant then goes on to offer food. She was inspired to grow a garden because of her stepmom. She told me that her stepmom did not have a huge garden, but that she always had a garden and always liked to be in it.

SUNFLOWER

TRIGGER WARNING: Mental illnesses including psychosis and mania

To me, sunflowers are some of the most beautiful and happy plants on this earth. I strive to be like a sunflower. Sunflowers are tall and they shine bright. They make me think of positivity, spreading light, and spreading love. I also really love the color yellow because it is a happy color. Sunflowers bloom in the summertime, which is my favorite time of the year. Young sunflowers constantly make an effort to face the sun. Like sunflowers, I believe one of my gifts is spreading light and happiness. I think that we all have it inside of ourselves to spread light.

A reason I chose to call this chapter what I did was because I have had friends tell me I am like a sunflower and like the color yellow. When I asked her about it, my friend Lauren told me, "You have always been yellow." I am also tall like the sunflowers, and she told me that I have a gentle and graceful way of doing things. This reminds me of the way sunflowers gently sway with the movement of air. My friend Logan described that I remind him of the color yellow because I am energetic but calming.

Just like the word "el sol", the word for sunflower is a masculine noun. Sunflower in Spanish is "el girasol". To me, sunflowers symbolize positivity. Positivity can be toxic, and as someone who works to be positive, I must be aware of toxic positivity. It is toxic positivity to tell someone to just smile when something very sad has just happened. We should let people feel their feelings. Another form of positivity that is toxic is lying about being happy. It is unhealthy to lie about being happy to others, but it may be even worse to lie about it to yourself. In my life, I have acted like I was fine even though I was not. I even lied to myself that I was more okay than I really was. Since I am naturally a very positive and optimistic person, it is sometimes difficult for me to understand that it does not always have to be that way. I had to learn that it was okay for me to show that I was sad or that I was struggling, and that it is not healthy to put on a happy face when the emotions underneath it are the opposite. I had to give myself permission to not always be a sunflower. There is no shame in needing help from others. Even the strongest of people need help from other people sometimes. In the end, we are all just human beings.

It is also toxic to plant sunflowers on top of poisonous roots. If the roots are poisonous, the sunflowers will be intertwined with that negativity. We should not act like everything is fine and just put a smile on our faces. It is time to be honest with others and ourselves. It is time to finally get to the roots of our issues and to truly heal. I did not heal from so many built-up roots in my life until 2020. In 2020, I started going to therapy. I journaled more than I ever have. I got to my roots.

I like to sit tall and still in meditations, just like the sunflowers stand tall in stillness when they are not dancing with the wind. There is something so magical about a sunflower field with and without the wind. When I am meditating, I am either still or moving. When I meditate, I try to put a smile on my face to welcome the happiness in the universe. Like the sunflowers, I aim to spread and receive light and love. When I am meditating, I feel close to the plants, all living things, and everything around me. I feel like a still and tall sunflower. I feel alive.

During my sophomore year of college, I took a marketing class that was based on marketing yourself, and essentially creating your own brand. In creating your own brand, you should figure out who you are and learn about yourself. Define exactly what your values are and always stay genuine. Figure out what your goals are and figure out how you would like to accomplish them. Find out what makes you unique, and you should not fight against it but instead take your natural abilities and your passions and combine them beautifully. Figure out what you would want other people to say about you if you were not in the room and ask yourself if you are treating others with kindness and in a positive way. Ask yourself if you would be happy being treated how you treat others.

Once you find the answers to these questions, you can create a brand of yourself. It seems a bit odd to talk about yourself as a brand, but it is about finding your values and staying true to them. It is about finding out who you really are and who you really want to be and finding ways to ease the gap between the two. Figure out what you are all about and what is truly important to you. You already have your own brand. A big part of your brand is how you treat others and how you make them feel.

Since this book has a lot of my own stories, I figured I should use a chapter to tell you about myself. This book is the story of me. As you can see on the back of the book, I am a normally functioning young woman who lost herself, found herself, and found mental healthiness. I am Mel. I go by Mel mostly, but my name is Melanie. I am an optimist. My hometown is a small town in Michigan called South Lyon. I have a brother and many cousins, and I am the youngest out of all my cousins. I wrote this book while taking a year off from Loyola University New Orleans, where I study finance. In my life, I have studied a lot of Spanish. From studying business, I found my interests in Human Resources and Finance and learned about the connection between these two parts and the business as a whole.

There were periods where I hated my business major when I was at my first university, Lindenwood University. I would ask myself why businesses do not care more about their employees or understand how important it is to make smart decisions with money with the happiness of people in mind. I believe that money cannot buy happiness in life, but that it does buy happiness in business. I also believe that the best way to treat people, including professionally and in business, is with kindness. People should be treated like plants. Through my studies in Spanish, I realized my passion for languages and writing as well as learning about different cultures and different foods. I also studied lots of Spanish literature, and that was when I learned about one of my biggest inspirations, Concepción Arenal. She carved the way for feminism in Spain. I studied Spanish for six years, and I would love to continue learning more about it.

I used to only go by Mel among swimmers, swim coaches, and the rest of the swimming community. "Mel" is the writer of this book. The name feels more me than "Melanie" does. Mel is positive, she smiles a lot, and she loves to laugh. I think that my personality shines the most when I am at the pool, and the water is a place that puts me at peace. When I am at the pool or going for a swim in a lake, I feel fully myself. I love wearing sundresses, being in the sunshine, singing, writing, spending time around plants and animals, and spreading light. Spreading light involves spreading positivity and happiness and lifting others with your words and actions. Doing these things makes me feel the most like me. It makes me feel true to myself to be like a sunflower, as sunflowers make people happy and in doing so, spread light.

A big part of my life is swimming. I started swimming competitively when I was six years old, but I have loved the water since the first time I got in a pool at the age of six months. My dad took me to a pool for the first time. I grew up loving Lake Michigan because it looks like an ocean. I have always loved how small I feel next to an ocean. I feel that same way when I stand looking at Lake Michigan now. I love lakes in general, and they became even more important to me in 2020.

In May of 2020, I had psychosis. After being hospitalized for psychosis, one of the only things I wanted to leave the house for was to go swimming. The first time I swam afterward, my mom took me, and I cried so many happy tears. I cannot even tell you how happy my mind was to have my body surrounded by the water and to hear the movement of it in my ears. My friends, Carolyn and Logan, helped me greatly because they knew exactly what I wanted to do when I was healing. I wanted to swim with them. The lake where they took me every time will now always have a very special place in my heart.

I had a manic episode in September of 2020. When I was in the hospital for it, there were some things that I wanted so badly. First, I wanted to hear more music. I have always loved music and singing. After I had gotten so tired of not hearing much music, as they only played music for us for about an hour or two, I started singing. I started going out right after meals when everyone had already finished eating but they still had some free time to stay outside in the partially blocked-off, screened-in area. One of the nurses brought in a microphone. Nurses and other patients sang after I sang. It was so happy, and everyone was dancing and laughing. People who I did not see smile much smiled when there was singing. I think singing lifts the spirits.

From all of this, I noticed how happy it made people to sing, and to hear other people singing. There is something so genuine about any kind of live music. There is also something so incredible about being in the sunlight. Standing out in that screened-in area at the behavioral health unit in the hospital, I felt the happiest I did for the whole time I was there. That, and the area right in front of my window were my happy places. I loved looking at the sunlight and doing a yoga sequence called sun salutations in the morning.

Sunny days and the summer make me so happy, and natural light coming in through a window makes me happy too. I taught a few of the friends I made at the hospital how to do sun salutations. One of them loved it so much and started doing them on his own every morning. Sun salutations are gentle and spiritual ways to start the day. I wanted to spread light to people in the hospital, including to the workers, and that is why I sang and did sun salutations.

Something else I realized during my time at that hospital was the lack of color. I wanted to see more colors so badly that I basically threw a fit to get crayons and a notebook. Once I had those things, I started drawing and coloring on blank white paper and giving them to my nurses and doctors. I drew ivy all over everything while I was there. While being in a place that lacked color, I realized how much colors meant to me.

Another thing that I missed so much while I was in the hospital for multiple days was being outside. I realized how much being outside meant to me when I was not able to do it. There have been many things in this life that have made me think about the importance of going outside. During quarantine, I was so thankful to get outside to go kayaking and walking. I was also thankful to have more time to go outside. Like many people, cold weather and the darkness that comes with it can really take a toll on my mood. During the winter of 2020, I decided to still go outside for walks, and it was the happiest Michigan winter that I can remember living. We are like plants, we need sunshine. We need to go outside.

I make sure there is enjoyment in every single day. Some daily and ordinary things that make me very happy are making coffee and preparing dinner. I also enjoy working out, even when all I am motivated to do is to go for a walk. To enjoy this life, we must give ourselves time to do so. In 2020, I learned how to be more of a morning person. I have always loved the nighttime but have not always loved the morning. I now see that the morning is a beautiful time to stay off my phone, read, meditate, and take in the day and the feelings that come with it.

Sunflowers taught me about who I want to be. I know that toxic positivity is an unhealthy thing and that I cannot always be like a sunflower. I need to recognize when I am not okay. I can usually try to be like the sunflowers, standing tall and happy with each other. Sunflower fields are a magnificent and happy sight. Sunflowers teach us about spreading light and happiness.

MANTRAS

TRIGGER WARNING: Emotional abuse, physical abuse, sexual abuse, narcissism, mental illness

"Know your worth."

A key in self-discovery, self-respect, and self-love is knowing who you are, as well as your worth. This is a mantra I have learned from others in different words, but never did I take it to heart as much as I did in 2020. You and I have worth. We have value. Because we have value, we have worth, meaning we are worthy. I believe that I am worthy of love, respect, and kindness. Do you know your worth? Do you have love and respect for yourself? If you always set the intention of being nice to others, respecting fellow human beings, and always trying your best, you will become more confident in who you are. You will learn to love yourself more because you will realize that your underlying intentions are good. Always trying your best is a delicate idea because your best will vary from day to day. It will be different if you are feeling down, bad, or anxious. The key is to forgive yourself for your different variations of your best. Forgiving yourself for imperfections is important to becoming and loving who you are.

There are many difficult times in life when we may question our own worth, such as at the end of any relationship, during a breakup, during family disagreements, or in polarizing political times. Always remember your worth. Sometimes people can be mean. People can lie to us, and they can betray us. In the end, the most important relationship we have is the one we have with ourselves. This brings me to an idea about feeling big and small, which is one of the chapters of this book. Feeling big and small is the idea that we are each our entire universe, but in the grand scheme of the universe, we are tiny. We are each minuscule percentages of the world population. Because of this, we may feel like the good we are doing for the world means nothing. We might think that we are so small and powerless that the changes we make will not really make a difference. An example of this is making environmentally conscious choices, such as bringing our own bags to the grocery store or walking when possible instead of driving. Too often, people feel like these small, good choices are not making a difference, or they say to themselves, "Nobody else is doing it, why does it matter if I do." This is the mentality that holds us back. Improving the environment to the level it needs will take the effort of millions. Even the smallest of changes can make a difference. Change is often good. Know that you can make a difference. We should all respect Mother Earth. Know your worth.

A thing that humans do much too often is judge each other. Humans judge others based on stories they hear, first impressions, or singular times that others wrong them or do something to undermine them. I disagree with the concept of "cancel culture." This is what happens when people do not give others a second chance after they make a mistake, and they say that a certain person is "cancelled". Second chances, and sometimes third and fourth chances, are beautiful. However, it comes to a point when you should stop forgiving someone when they have done enough wrong. No person should ever be held to a standard of perfection because no one is perfect. No human is entirely bad or entirely good, either. The idea of putting a label of "good person" and "bad person" is much too black and white; it is not that simple. It is hard to admit but even the meanest of people may have some good to them. After we, individually or as a society, give them this label of bad or evil, the good is insanely difficult to see.

We are human beings, and we make mistakes. Because human beings have such powerful memories, we hold grudges against others. We judge ourselves and hold grudges against ourselves, too. We can remind ourselves over and over of the wrongs that we or others did, and we can remind others over and over of the wrongs they did. Often before even meeting someone, we judge them based on what we have heard. We can instead try to form our own opinions.

Sometimes there is a reason for this judgement because some people abuse other people. Forming any relationship with a person accused of emotional, physical, or sexual abuse should be done with extreme caution, and it might be better if a relationship with a person like this is avoided completely. Sometimes, that person could be a family member or a close tie. In my opinion, it is healthy to avoid those accused by someone we trust or those who abused us personally. In many cases, it is best to avoid someone who has been accused of abuse, especially if it is serial. The tricky part about people is that some lie about being victims of abuse. It takes time to see if people are honest people.

Some people cannot stop lying. Pathological liars can tell lies with the intention to seem like better people or like victims, even if they are not truthfully that. Liars who cannot seem to stop lying may have underlying issues that cause this, such as anxiety or low self-esteem. People like this might actually need someone to tell them their worth and remind them that they have a light in them since they do not see it themselves and think they must lie. I have been friends with liars before, and it is difficult to see it in the beginning. They can often seem like nice and honest people. I wish I could go back and help them. I wish I could tell them the things that I loved about them when I first knew them, to tell them that they have a light inside of them and need to let it shine, and to tell them that they have good to offer.

It is not healthy to return to people who wronged us deeply, or who have wronged us many times. Sometimes, we must let people go. Knowing our self-worth can help us understand when a relationship is dragging us down more than lifting us up. We must learn to be critical of our friendships and relationships to avoid the destruction and pain caused by pathological liars and abusers. We must also learn to love ourselves enough to escape this treatment or to never accept it in the first place. We need to learn when a relationship is no longer serving us well. There is a remarkable power in the words "no" and "goodbye."

With this being said, I am obsessed with finding the good in others. I believe that there must be some good in every human since I believe that we are born with love and taught to hate. Some people tell occasional lies without much intention or because of their hate for conflict. Human beings naturally make mistakes. I believe in forgiveness. I became this way because I hold myself to a high standard, and I have finally learned that holding people and yourself to a high standard is completely different than holding everyone to a standard of perfection. Holding others and yourself to a high standard is acceptable, but perfection is unattainable and unhealthy. There must always be room for error. The reason that we hold other humans to a standard of perfection is because we hold ourselves to our own, or society's own, idea of perfection. Think about how it feels when you judge yourself over and over for the same mistake. Next, think about how it feels when someone else, especially someone you are close to, reminds you over and over of your mistakes. Judgements, including self-judgements and judgments from others, slowly diminish our sense of self-worth.

I struggle greatly with perfectionism and the anxiety that comes with it. I have learned that if you do things very well but always give yourself room for error, you will be much happier. The standard of perfection is much too high. You are happier when you are easier on yourself, staying positive, and not judging yourself excessively. There is a book that has had a very positive influence on my life, and that book is *The Four Agreements* by Don Miguel Ruiz. *The Four Agreements* is a personal growth and self-help book. Ruiz explains four seemingly simple agreements that people can make with themselves and bases these agreements on ancient Toltec wisdom. The fourth agreement is to always do your best. Ruiz states, "Under any circumstance, always do your best, no more and no less. But keep in mind that your best is never going to be the same from one moment to the next. Everything is alive and changing all the time, so your best will sometimes be high quality, and other times it will not be as good," (Ruiz 85). [1] The key is to always do your best, and if you do so, you should never judge yourself or compare yourself to others or to perfection because your best is something only you can understand. Setting a standard of perfection is too often unattainable. Know your worth, but do not aim to be perfect.

My very good friend that I met in my first year in college, Matias, repeated and still repeats some very valuable mantras. I was instantly drawn to Matias from the first conversation that we ever had over lunch in the Evans dining hall at Lindenwood University. I could see myself in him, as well as a bright light coming from inside him. I recently told him that I did not learn to take his advice fully until two years after hearing it over and over, but the things he said played over and over in my mind until they finally became something I could understand. He would always say, "You are nice, but you need to learn respect." I took this as him telling me that I needed to learn to respect others more. I took it as a negative about me, but what he meant was not what I thought he meant. What Matias was saying was that I needed to respect myself more. He wanted me to realize my worth. He would also repeat, "You need to be confident." Matias is a beautiful person, inside and out, and he has a ridiculous amount of confidence. I now understand that Matias knew his worth from an early age. He knew that he was nice, and he knew that he liked the person he was. He had respect for himself. He knew that his opinion of himself, as well as the opinions of his close friends and family, were the most important, and that opinions of other people outside of the ones who truly matter were simply noise. Matias taught me about knowing my worth.

"We rise by lifting others." - Robert G. Ingersoll

To me, this mantra is about seeing the good in others and helping them to see it too. After learning the mantra, "We rise by lifting others," I wrote it down multiple times, and then I started to live by it. When I was younger, my mom always said, and still says, "Lead by example." She would tell this to me and my brother often. My mom constantly ensured that John and I were doing our best and becoming nice and respectful people. From a young age, everyone knew that John would be an engineer. He now is an accomplished civil engineer. He set high bars for me, being the valedictorian of his high school class and getting his undergraduate and graduate degrees in civil engineering at an accelerated pace. I wanted to be like him, but I had no desire to do exactly what he did. I was me, not him. I was fiercely independent at a young age. I liked things done a specific way, and I liked to do things for myself. I still am this way. However, I was not confident in my leadership abilities until recently. I was afraid of them, I think, and afraid of the way that I could influence people if I stepped into the role of it. I realized the power of leading by example, and that example is to be uplifting, caring, hardworking, and positive. I learned to listen to my mom's words.

My best friend, Carolyn, has taught me so much. We met when I was five years old, and we joined the same swim team when we were six. That was when I began swimming. I often say that Carolyn and I practically raised each other. Carolyn planted in me the idea that leaders are made, not born because she showed me that people must work on themselves constantly as leaders. People can be naturally good leaders, but the ones who work on themselves can truly be great. She taught me about leadership, and she also taught me about what to look for in a good friend. She embodies the definition of a great friend, and she has done it for almost my entire life.

Carolyn noticed before I did that I have the power to lead by example and that I could be a leader in general. Carolyn also pointed out to me my strengths and she would motivate and push me when she knew I could achieve the goals I was striving for. She is my best friend. She knows what I am capable of because she has seen it all. She has been around since I started swimming, so she is always able to give me some encouraging words with it, even when we are both struggling. Carolyn swam on a NCAA D1 team and had quite a few accomplishments there. Even though we were on different college teams, she met my previous team, and I met her team. We know the kind of people and the environments that we have been surrounded by. When we were on the same high school team, Carolyn was one of my main motivators every day.

I learned the power of positivity in leadership when I started leading shifts at an ice cream shop. I worked there during summers starting the summer before my senior year of high school. I learned that I could create an amazing and fun atmosphere if I turned on music that made me want to dance and made to-do lists that left no question of what my expectations were for my coworkers. My managers taught me this, and they taught me the power of communicating exactly what I wanted done. Something I learned from my second manager at the ice cream shop, Alivia, was that a person in a leadership role has no power unless they are also working hard and not just imposing their power on others so they can sit back and do nothing. This manager was one of the most hardworking people that I have ever met. She led with positivity, organization, and lists. Lists show exactly what needs to be done. A manager will struggle to lead effectively if they cannot communicate effectively. If a manager fails to communicate and fails to work hard themselves, they will struggle to inspire and uplift their employees.

Not only is leading by example important, but it is also important to lead using your own special set of traits and ideas. Much of this book is based on the empowerment of people, and especially the empowerment of women. About half of the people who need to be uplifted are women, so this book contains chapters to make women feel powerful. There is something incredible about women, and I believe that everyone can learn from great inspiring female leaders. I also think that anyone can lead with a feminine approach.

Being optimistic makes life better. Only seeing and dwelling on the negatives takes away from the positives. Sharing optimism and positivity with others may be a gift. It may help people realize that they are just going through a bad day or a bad time, not a bad life. The things we say and show to others are contagious. We must not share toxic positivity, which can happen when we tell a person something like "just cheer up" instead of listening and understanding when something difficult goes on in someone's life. We cannot forget that we do not need to be happy all the time, but we can always try to stay positive and optimistic.

A way to practice optimism and positivity is with gratitude. It can feel great to practice gratitude for ourselves and our bodies. I keep a gratitude journal to write things down that I am thankful for. Practicing gratitude reminds me of all the good things in my life. I also practice gratitude by telling people when I am thankful for them or their help. Think of how nice it feels to be thanked and pay it forward. Always remember to be positive and remember that people do not forget how you make them feel.

Another way we rise by lifting others is by helping them realize and understand their own worth. We can tell them the things we love about them. Not only can we tell them, but we can also remind and show them how much we appreciate them. We can give them compliments and thank them for being who they are. Within every one of us, there is light and there is love.

It was my mom who taught me how satisfying and anxiety-reducing it is to create a list and check off the tasks on the list. Creating a list and accomplishing the things on the list is a form of goal setting. I believe in setting goals and physically writing them down with paper and a writing utensil. When you see your goals over and over, you will start to manifest them. Likewise, when you see or hear a mantra that resonates with you repeatedly, you will start to live by it. Goals and mantras are ways of uplifting ourselves. I learned the power of goal setting when I was 10 years old, and I created a swimming journal. In my swimming journal, I would write down inspirational quotes, small goals for practices, and the times I wanted to accomplish. I would also write as well as tell others, including my family, friends, and coaches, that I was going to win the state meet.

I knew that I was unnaturally tall for my age and that I had the wingspan to go along with it, and because of this, I knew I could do it. My coach would tell me that I should worry more about the time I wanted to achieve, and if I worked hard enough and visualized myself going this time-goal, the rest would fall into place. With this in mind, I wrote down times that I knew would be the fastest out of any of the other 10-year-old girls in the state for the 100-meter and 50-meter breaststroke. When the state meet came along, I was excited and barely even nervous because I knew I was well prepared. My mom and dad took me to get lunch before going to the pool, and lunch was per my request – chicken nuggets with a side of ranch. Next, they drove me to the pool, and I won the state meet. At the age of 10, I had learned the power of writing down attainable goals and taking the steps to manifest them.

When humankind finally universally recognizes that we rise by lifting others we will be unstoppable. We must also learn to uplift ourselves and to know that we can have high standards for the way people treat us. If we are unhappy with our situations, we can change them. When we can uplift the people we love, we can help them realize things they do not realize about themselves. We can uplift ourselves with positive self-talk, surrounding ourselves with people who truly make us feel good, and by learning how to set goals on what we really want and being able to attain them.

You are not a half.

I think a lot of people think of themselves as needing others, or one particular other, to feel whole. You are allowed to be single. You do not have to have children, and you do not have to get married. You can spend your life essentially alone, and that would be completely okay. We are not halves. We are not even 90% us; you are 100% you. You get to make your own decisions. You are the only one you will spend the rest of your life with. Make the relationship you have with yourself the best one that you have. Do things for yourself that are kind, such as drinking enough water, meditating, and pursuing your passions. Fully learn yourself and your interests and ways of doing everything. Learn your weaknesses, too, and try to work on them. However, never forget that you are not a half.

When I envision myself in the future, I live alone in the mountains, and I have two big dogs. One of these dogs is a Samoyed, and she is so beautiful. The other is a Golden Retriever or a Bernese Mountain Dog, and she is beautiful too. I do not imagine a man living there with me. This does not go to say that I could never imagine myself in a relationship or a marriage, but it is just not how I picture it in my head. I imagine doing things for myself and often by myself, since I do not see myself as a half or a part. I am whole on my own. I imagine my dogs and I and the view of the mountains. I imagine myself with a blanket and a good book or a journal sitting on the couch looking out at the view.

I know that we are not halves, and I know that we are all whole people who do not need someone else to complete us. People too often forget how much they are worth, and they think that other people's opinions matter too much. We also often easily forget that we can be single, and that it is not bad at all to do so. At the end of a relationship, always remember that you are so much more than a half. You are a whole. When a relationship ends, you can focus on bettering yourself, the relationship with you, and the relationships with those who make you feel loved.

We are not obligated to have children and we do not have to get married. We are whole all by ourselves. We are individuals, and we do not have to sacrifice that if we do not want to. We are allowed to spend this life mostly alone if that is what we prefer. We must keep in mind, however, that we are like the trees, meaning we can work together to make this existence better for all around us. Sometimes, it is nice to have other people to share this experience with.

Make this world a better place with your existence.

I think that we can be whatever we want to see more of in the world. Personally, I want to see more female and feminine leaders in the world, so I want to be one. I also want to spread light. Maybe you want to be the parent, the manager, the kind person, the helpful person, the nurse, or the friend you wish existed. Whatever it is that you care about or feel passionate about, let yourself fully embody that. Grow and become the person you want to be.

I had a large sticker on the wall of my childhood bedroom that said, "Be the change you wish to see in the world," which I recently discovered was a paraphrased version of a longer quote from Mahatma Gandhi. I cannot remember exactly why I loved these words so much, but I know that I saw it repeatedly and because of that, I thought about it often. Thinking about bringing something to the world and knowing that we have the power to create change, to spread love, and to share light, gave, and still gives me a powerful and beautiful feeling. Even though we are so tiny in the grand scheme of things, we can make more of a difference in this world than we know.

I want to write about mantras and their power. I am choosing to do this in this section specifically because this is one of my oldest mantras. Mantras can block out intrusive thoughts and can become a part of meditation. Mantras bring peace by allowing us to focus on a singular word or a small grouping of words that mean something to us, which brings us to the present moment. When people meditate, as well as when they practice the repetition of a mantra, they can become more present, calm, and focused. We can release the chaos going through our minds, including the thoughts about what happened in our day, what is stressing us out, and what is making us anxious. Mantras can help us feel centered, inspired, strong, and confident. Mantras can change our lives.

Treat people with kindness.

This is a self-help and self-love book and part of helping and loving yourself is being kind to yourself. Not only should you treat yourself kindly, but you should treat others with kindness too. My brother John is one of the kindest people I have ever met. He is willing to go out of his way to do nice gestures for people, and he always thinks about others. John embodies always trying to treat people with kindness. Part of treating people with kindness is treating people how they want to be treated, and John does just that. He cares about others and makes people feel good. Having a brother or a sibling can be like having a built-in best friend. John is my best friend and a person I look up to. I look up to the way he treats me and others, and I look up to his creativity and intelligence.

I spoke to my brother John about this mantra, and he said that you cannot know exactly how people want to be treated unless you are them. You are best off treating them with kindness and cautiously. You must keep in mind that people have different reactions to everything and what they want might not match up with what you want. Therefore, you can try to be cautious and careful with how you treat others. If somebody does tell you how they want to be treated or what they want you to do in certain situations, you should try to adapt to it. You can adapt to how people respond to you. If you do not know how someone wants you to treat them, the best way to treat them is kindly, carefully, and cautiously.

I asked John about his mantras and one of them he told me was "Keep on keeping on." This goes along the lines of another mantra he lives by, which is "Just keep going until you make it." John is one of the hardest workers that I know. He has been a hard worker for as long as I can remember. We swam on the same team together, and John encouraged others with his hard work. He was also a very hardworking student. John has endurance. He has the will to succeed at whatever he sets his mind to. He believes that if you work hard, there is no guarantee that you will do well, but there is a much higher likelihood of it. He told me that working smartly is sometimes more important than working hard. The best solution can sometimes be the simplest one.

Working smartly instead of just hard reminds me of the difference between treating people how you want to be treated and how they want to be treated. When possible, it is better to treat people how they want to be treated if you can understand it or if they tell you. Just like working smartly, treating people how they want to be treated takes a lot of thought. Sometimes, you need to take a step back and think hard about what you are doing. Doing this will help you be more mindful.

Another one of John's mantras is "Try to experience as many new things as you can." You will find things you do not like, and you will find things you do like. Traveling is very good because it opens your eyes to new places and new experiences. John finds it interesting to see how the rest of the world is organized. He believes in traveling not just for the pursuit of pleasures but instead to see other approaches to the daily world and the way others live. When you go somewhere new, doing mundane things like getting on the subway or going to the grocery store can show you the way people in a different part of the world live. The way you live your life is just one of seven billion.

John believes that traveling should be about immersing yourself. He also loves seeing the great scenery and trying the delicious food, but he thinks that the most important part of traveling is to see the different ways of existing. John's favorite place he has traveled to was Mexico City. I went with John to Mexico City, and we quickly learned how beautiful and cared for the city was. We saw lovely flowers and cute dogs, we ate incredibly flavorful food, and we climbed the pyramids of Teotihuacán. You can absorb things from people in your daily life and from traveling. You can learn to honor the strengths and perspectives of others. You can learn something from everyone you meet, and you should. One of the most interesting things you can do is see something you have never seen before.

Traveling and learning about others helps people learn about themselves. Traveling teaches people about diversity and the beauty of having differences between people. When traveling, we should aim to respect everyone and treat people kindly, always. Traveling is about honoring that we are different and wanting to understand what life is like in a different part of the world. It is about experiencing something new, and it is about seeing a place you have never seen before. This world is so big, there are so many people to meet, and there is so much to see. It would be a shame not to travel somehow.

Traveling can be done in many ways. It can be movement, but it can also be done inside of our minds. We can travel by daydreaming, reading, seeing pictures, looking at maps, and imagining. We can also travel by meeting and learning about people and their lives. We can travel interpersonally. You do not have to go far to be able to travel and from traveling we can learn about people and ourselves. We can travel by going to bookstores and libraries. We can approach every single day with a mindset that we are traveling with a curious and absorbent mind.

In this life, we create much of our reality. We make choices every day about how to treat people and what to say. We have the option to be rude and disrespectful to others and ourselves, but we also have the option to be kind and respectful. We simply must make that choice. Never exploring is a choice one can make. We can travel to learn and to grow as people, and we can travel to learn about diversity and the way people go about their daily lives in different parts of the world. We have so much love to offer to others, all we must do is offer it. We also have the option to always try to be kind. I think we should choose kindness and love.

I love you.

This mantra is mainly about self-love. Our sense of self-worth, and our amount of self-love, determine how we will be loved. These two things also determine how we will allow others to treat us. If we do not love and respect ourselves, we will not expect a high level of love or respect from others. In turn, we are not able to fully love and respect someone else if we do not see our worth and if we do not love ourselves. It is possible to love others and to not love oneself, but the love will become so much deeper and so much more beautiful once we learn to be at peace with ourselves, to appreciate ourselves and our efforts, and once we honor every single thing about ourselves.

I believe in showing people love through actions and words besides just saying, "I love you." I think we can show our love with hugs, making time for people, and giving them undivided attention with this time. We can say "I love you" without actually saying it by simply treating people how they want to be treated. We can pay close attention to people's feelings and the words they say, we can send people songs that remind us of them, we can call and check in on them. Other ways we can show "I love you" is by arranging activities with people that you will both enjoy, making sure they get home safely, and reminding them of the things you love about them.

Sometimes we need others to tell us the good things about us before we realize them ourselves, and if we realize them ourselves it feels good when others reinforce them. For example, if we always try to be nice to others, it feels good when people say we are nice. If we try hard to put together an outfit and do our hair, it feels very good when someone compliments us. I think that compliments of our personalities are so much more rewarding than compliments of our appearance, but any compliment can make us feel good. Never forget to compliment your friends and loved ones, as it will help them love themselves more and become more confident in the things that they should have confidence in.

There are similarities between self-love, a positive thing, and narcissism and over-confidence, which are negative things. Where is the line drawn between loving yourself and loving yourself too much? I think it is about how we treat others. If we love ourselves about equally to how we love others, and if we always treat each other with kindness, loving ourselves is a very good thing. If we love ourselves to a point that we do not know how to really love others because all our love is for us, that would not be a very good thing. I have always been curious about something when it comes to narcissism, and the thing I am curious about is how and where the line is drawn between being a narcissist and not being a narcissist. I think about the negative connotations that come with being overly confident, but then realize that it is admirable to be confident, just not overly confident. Similarly, it is beautiful to love yourself, but it is not beautiful to be a narcissist. We learn the lovely words "I love you" early in our lives. We then learn how to say them to ourselves later in life, but some never learn to say or think them. Maybe it is because we are told by society that loving ourselves a lot is wrong.

We strive for perfect bodies, perfect diets, perfect relationships, perfect jobs, and perfect lives. In this pursuit, we forget that we are living. We forget that human beings make mistakes all the time, and we forget that everyone has imperfections even if they do not show them. On social media, we see people posting pictures and updates and wish our lives were more like theirs.

We see people with bodies that we want so badly, but bodies are simply not made the same. We have different metabolisms, genetics, bone structures, and heights. Even if we all ate the same things and did the same workouts, we still would not have the same bodies. These are always going to be our bodies for as long as we live, and instead of thinking about all the things our body does not do or the way we wished it looked, we can always practice gratitude for all the things it does. We can exercise, even if it is just something small like going for a walk, we can eat fruits and vegetables, and we can get a proper amount of sleep. We can eat, exercise, and go about our lives with the intention to be healthy and feel good, not to be perfect. Instead of looking at our legs and thinking about how big they are, we can look at our legs and think of the incredible things they can do. Instead of looking in the mirror and calling our stomach fat or being disappointed in it, think about how your stomach lets you know when you are hungry, when you are full, and when you do not feel well. Our stomachs and legs do so much for us. Thank them.

This all ties into the idea that we must know our worth, but it also relates to rising by lifting others, another mantra. We all have an internal voice, and the voice inside of us is sometimes meaner and more unforgiving than anyone else. The voice inside of us can tell us that we are not good enough, and when we look in the mirror that voice sometimes tells us that we are fat and ugly. Our internal voice reminds us repeatedly of our imperfections. We must learn to replace this internal negativity with internal positivity. We can raise ourselves by fighting off the negative self-talk that goes on inside our heads.

We can tell that negative voice that it is wrong, just like we could tell someone we love that the people who are being mean to them are wrong. We can learn to look in the mirror and say to ourselves, "I love you, despite your imperfections." Once we can truthfully do this and mean it, we can stop chasing a standard that has no end. We will find love and acceptance for ourselves and our bodies, and we will start to enjoy life so much more.

"And I said to my body softly, 'I want to be your friend.' It took a long breath and replied, 'I have been waiting my whole life for this."
- Nayyirah Waheed

I have also learned that negative comments from others are often reflections of their own insecurities, and it is possible to become immune to the negative feelings that come from those comments by simply knowing your worth and knowing that you are trying your best. If your intentions are always good, and you always try to treat people with kindness, make sure you remember it when someone says something to you that makes you feel bad. If you allow the negative comments to be meaningful to you, they will turn into negative self-talk. You might even believe things that are not true about you. It takes practice to ignore these negative comments from others, but you can decide that they are not correct. The people with opinions about you that matter are not strangers or people who barely know you. You are worth more and deserve more than the comments that make you feel bad.

I hear people hating on themselves together. I hear groups of young women bash their own bodies over casual conversations like it is a competition to hate themselves more than anyone else hates themselves. "I hate my legs," one girl says, and another says, "Your legs are so much better than my legs. I hate my arms too." It turns into a cycle of hate. We can finally end this cycle and say to each other, "Your legs do so much for you, and you should thank them. Besides, they are beautiful, just like you." When we hear someone hating on themselves, we should try to uplift them. We can turn the conversation into something positive and stop the cycle of hate.

We have so much love to offer. We have love we can give ourselves, our friends, our family, and to people we do not even know. We especially should love ourselves. Someone may have narcissistic qualities, but they might stem from something other than being an actual narcissist. An example of a quality that might seem like narcissism even though it might not be is confidence. It can sometimes seem that people are offended or confused when someone else has a lot of confidence, or that we are expected to not have a lot of confidence. Confidence is so very important. Confidence is about loving yourself and being proud of yourself and your efforts. Additionally, it takes confidence to love yourself. To love yourself, you must learn to love your own company, not stretch yourself too thin while giving to others, forgive yourself, and take good care of yourself. I learned confidence from swimming, the people I love, and from myself.

You cannot truly support someone unless you know how to support yourself. People who have overcome huge obstacles themselves, or who understand struggles and support people through theirs, tend to be the ones with the best advice. I have learned this from friends who I know have gone through immensely difficult times, and the main people in my life who remind me of this are Carolyn and Grant.

In this book, I wrote about people. I wrote about the people I know, the stories they have told me, and the things I have learned from them. There are some people and some stories that I did not write about, but that does not mean that they have not influenced me greatly and it does not mean that those people have not made my life better, because they have. It does not mean that I do not have love for them. I believe that people are what make this life so beautiful and that every single person we have met has shaped us in some way. We would not be who we are without the people we have around us.

Someone who has taught me so much about uplifting others is my friend, Grant. Grant supported me when I first started to have struggles with my mental health, and we were there for each other through the thick and thin of our freshman year of college. Like many freshmen, my living situation was far from ideal. At that point in my life, I did not understand the beauty of goodbye, and I heavily searched for validation from others. When I did not get that validation, or when someone would dislike me or say mean things to me, I would take it very hard, and I struggled with that.

I convinced myself that because my living situation with other girls was not great, I was much more fit to live alone than to live with roommates. I felt that I would be better off living alone the next year, and my sophomore year turned out to be one of the best years of my life. It turned out so great even though I had such low hopes for it, and even though I shed many tears while driving to Missouri with my parents at the end of the summer of 2018. My two best friends I had made freshman year, Matias and Grant, had both transferred to new universities after the first year. Not only had my friends left, but I was also going to be living on my own, and I was very nervous about all of it.

Living alone taught me all the things I love about solitude and about being in the company of just myself. In a section where I am writing about how others can uplift us and how we can uplift others, it is fitting to also point out the importance of solitude. When we spend time alone, we learn about ourselves, we learn about our desires, and we can think deeply and possibly be creative. Therefore, spending time in solitude can lead to us having a better relationship with ourselves, which in turn helps us better our relationships with others. Living alone showed me how essential it was to have time alone and to have a place where I could be alone. I realized there was no way I could uplift others if I could not uplift myself. I also realized that I needed to find validation within myself.

I spoke with Grant while writing this book and we talked about solitude. He told me that he believes it is very important and that we need to have things that are our own that we enjoy doing alone. Grant loves computers. He explained that he loves problem-solving computer issues because it keeps his mind thinking and fresh. The time he has with computers is very important and necessary to him. He has noticed that he does not have friends who are as interested in computers as he is, but because of this, it truly became his thing. Spending time alone and especially having something we love to do alone is a self-care practice. Practicing self-care is a way to say "I love you" to ourselves.

Another place Grant enjoyed solitude in his life was when he was a diver. Through diving, Grant learned about fighting his self-doubt and controlling his own thoughts. Being in tune with his emotions and trusting himself makes Grant feel closer to himself. Diving was an escape for him. It is a very individual sport which made it a place where he had time to himself. Grant told me that his favorite coaches understood that he dove because he loved it and that he dove for himself.

Although Grant believes that solitude is important, he pointed out the differences between solitude and isolation. There are differences between solitude and isolation and differences between independence and loneliness. Solitude and independence are more positive than isolation and loneliness. Even though solitude and independence are important, you cannot do everything alone. We need to talk to each other, and sometimes we need help from each other. We are social beings.

When we process what happens in this life, we often need to talk about it. Grant and I spoke about how it is hard for some people to speak positively within our own minds. Even if we are very positive on the outside, we might have negative thoughts on the inside. If we talk about those negative thoughts, we address them. We need to experience the good things in life while acknowledging that the bad things exist. We can talk about the bad, and it is very healthy to get it out when negativity is trapped within us. It is so important to address negative emotions and understand that we do not control what happens, but we can control how we react to it.

Grant's main mantra is, "Be true to yourself". Accept yourself for who you really are and accept yourself for all the things you like and the hobbies that you have. If you are true to yourself, you will be happier. You cannot make yourself into someone you are not. Being true to yourself also involves being honest with yourself. There is no use in lying to yourself. It also includes being critical of yourself and your decisions since every decision you make impacts who you will become. You should be true to yourself by not lying to yourself that you are happy if you are not. You can get yourself out of unhappy situations and unhappy phases. You can make changes in your life, as you are the one who is writing it.

Carolyn was there for me after both of my visits to the psychiatric ER. My friends Carolyn, Morgan, and Logan were the only people I saw other than my parents after everything that happened the first time, and they helped me more than I can ever explain. After my first visit, when I had psychosis, I was not capable of much and was scared by small things. I did not trust anyone, and I had a fear of leaving my house. I thought that I was going to be kicked out of the house, which was an idea that I got somehow based on no evidence at all. Carolyn came back to Michigan from Ohio when she heard I had been to the hospital. She was there for me when I needed it most. Carolyn has been my best friend since I was about five years old, and in ways, I feel like we had a lot to do with the raising of each other and with each other's growth as people. She is a little bit older than me, so Carolyn met me when I was five and she was six. We met on a tee-ball team and when I turned six, we joined a swim team together.

I look for Carolyn in others. She is my highest standard of a friend because I have been friends with her for so much of my life. Carolyn knows me almost as well as I know myself. When I meet people who have similar characteristics to Carolyn, I am attracted to them as friends. I noticed similarities to her in my Loyola teammate, Kamy, from the minute I met her. Kamy was the leader of my recruiting trip as a middle-of-the-year junior transfer. Kamy was also just a very upbeat and smiley person, and I knew I liked that from the minute I met her because that is how my best friend is.

Another girl who reminded me a lot of Carolyn when I became friends with her is Josey. Josey is one of the most caring and supportive people I have ever met, and she is also one of the best listeners. Josey's friends explain her as the type of person that people want to be around. Josey loves to try new things, and her energy is very attractive. She quickly reminded me of Carolyn in the way she cares and the way she listens.

I became friends with Josey during my sophomore year at Lindenwood, and she reminded me what it was like to find a friend soulmate. Soulmates do not come around often, but when they do, they can make life so sweet and so good. In fact, Matias was good friends with Josey when Matias and I were freshmen, but I had only talked with her a little. Matias knew I was nervous to be going back to school without him and Grant, and he told me I should talk to Josey. It turned out to be one of the best friendships I have ever had. Josey always supports me, always uplifts me, and we have a fantastic and fun time whenever we are together.

Josey and I have the kind of friendship where we can go to the grocery store or run errands together and have the most fun time possible while doing it. One of our favorite things to do together is to drive, ideally with the windows down, while watching the sunset and listening to our favorite songs. We were on the swim team together, and the bond between swimmers is something that I have always found to be so special. Josey would pick me up for morning swim practice, wait outside my door at 5:05 am, and I would play songs that I thought she would like on the way to practice. I think that music is one of the greatest ways to connect with people. I also think that having friends is one of the most enriching parts of the human experience.

Finally, I was reminded of Carolyn, and of Josey, when I met my friend Maddie at Loyola. I have only known Maddie for a short time, but she is also one of my friend soulmates. I appreciate the way she is able to listen and remember so well. I also love Maddie's free and lighthearted spirit that goes along with mine so easily. That is the part of her that reminds me of Josey the most. The thing about Maddie that reminds me of Carolyn is their mutual love for loungewear and their amazing positive personalities.

I believe in the words "I love you." I believe in mantras and the power that they possess. My mantras are: know your worth, we rise by lifting others, you are not a half, make this world a better place with your existence, treat people with kindness, and I love you. I love all those words. I love meditating while saying those words. I live by them, and I think it could improve the lives of many to understand these mantras. I also believe in treating people like plants.

REAL HUMAN CONNECTIONS

TRIGGER WARNING: Psychosis, mania

I believe in connecting with each other. Real human connections are rare, deep, and genuine. They are not easy to find in today's age, especially with the access to social media and phones that we have. It is easy to ignore the strangers we pass and to simply look at our screens. The issue with these little screens is that they are not real life. The pictures we see of others and their seemingly perfect lives do not tell us who they are. The photos do not tell us about their personality and how they treat others, and they do not tell us about the person's imperfections. The way we find out these things is by actually getting to know somebody. We naturally chase after love. We may want to feel love from friends, family, or romantically. We all need love. Love is a basic human need and something we need to be able to grow. We can find love in ourselves, but we cannot find a sense of belonging and feeling accompanied if we do not find love with others. We need real human connections.

Have you ever thought about what it is exactly that makes you feel inspired? Have you found what you need to do to feel creative and fulfilled? For me, I am inspired by people and their stories. I am also inspired by nature, music, and books. We are all inspired somehow. I asked a few friends how they feel inspired, and some of the responses were that they feel inspired by exercising, drinking coffee, cooking, and calling or seeing a friend. People can be inspired by looking at something with a glass half full and optimistic approach. Those who are positive and have faith and hope are not only inspired people, but they also are inspiring to others.

Phones make it harder to truly connect with others, and I think that too many people use their phones too much. I think there is something so amazing about putting my phone away for a little while. It gives me time to think and breathe. I do not have to worry about responding at that moment or worry about what to say. When I put my phone away, I can either fully connect with others, or I can fully connect with myself.

I suggest putting your phone away during social experiences especially if it is between you and one other person, and I suggest putting it away when you are on your own, too. Many of us are much too worried about replying to text messages promptly. Texts are not calls. They serve a different purpose. You can reply to a text when you are ready to. The most important information is typically not sent as a text message. Think about the important conversations that you have had in your life and think about how many of those were in person or over the phone, not through texting. It is a much more valuable use of your time with other people to simply put your phone down.

I also suggest trying to put your phone away when you are alone, too. Something that I love to do is to go to the park with a backpack and to put my phone away in it. Sometimes I put on a playlist while I walk, and sometimes I simply pay attention to my surroundings. I also like to do this while walking to class, where it would normally seem fitting to take out my phone and scroll through social media or answer texts. Instead, I like to leave my phone in my bag. I look around at what is going on and pay attention to the world around me. These are forms of meditation and mindfulness. As I explain in the Meditations chapter, meditating is not just about staring at a wall or closing your eyes and trying to force all the thoughts out of your mind. It can be these things, but meditation is so much more. It can also be done by focusing on something closely, such as something going on or one of the thoughts that comes to mind. Meditation is about awareness and tranquility.

Finally, I also put my phone down in the morning. I do not look at it for about an hour after I wake up. I like to feel my emotions, think about whatever comes to my mind, and try to start the day off right. If you check your phone the minute you wake up in the morning, you allow the thoughts of others to impact your day when it has barely even started.

After I had psychosis, I decided to start picking up my phone after doing other things, such as stretching and making myself coffee and a nice breakfast. When I had psychosis, and for about two or three weeks after leaving the hospital, I did not even look at my phone. I did not know if people were calling or texting, I did not take any pictures, and only a few of my friends knew what was happening. My phone was completely overwhelming to me, and I was basically incapable of using it anyway. I learned something from all of it, but one thing I took with me is that phones were not just overwhelming to me when I had psychosis, but that they can be very overwhelming daily. It is often a good thing not to feel overwhelmed.

Phones are not people. You can call people from a phone, but phones do not give us the same human to human connection and interaction that we can have in person with each other. We need to see each other outside of a screen. Because of the pandemic, video conferencing and calling happened more than ever before. I feel that there is a great loss when so much is done over the phone and through the computer. Some of the things we lose are body language and an in-person greeting and goodbye. It is so much easier to keep track of time when using a computer or a phone to converse, which makes it more difficult to lose oneself in the conversation. We lived lives that had more 3D interaction before the pandemic, but the circumstances made so many 3D interactions into 2D ones. I believe in putting away my 2D devices often. I also believe there is something so different about a real human interaction that cannot be perfectly substituted with a screen.

A study from the University of Gothenburg in Sweden showed the links between phone use and the effects on stress, depression, and sleep. [2] Over 4,000 young adults of the ages 20 to 24 participated in this yearlong study. The researchers predicted that the study would show a negative effect on health, and more particularly mental health, with more phone use. As anticipated, the study did show a direct relationship between high-level phone use and reports of depression. This fact is concerning, especially today when there is such an increase in mental health issues, and that during the pandemic many people spent more time on their phones. It is also concerning because many people feel as though they have no control over how much they use their phones and struggle to limit their behavior. Many people suffer from the fear of being without their phone, which is referred to as nomophobia. People can also feel like they are getting a notification even though in reality they are not, causing them to check their phone even more.

The University of Gothenburg's study focused on more than just the quantity of phone use and additionally reviewed the effects of "high accessibility" stress. High accessibility stress is about how much a person stresses about being accessible. Many participants reported feeling guilty when they were unable to return all calls and texts and reported that a major stressor for them was to not be available. Accessibility stress is also about how much a person is disturbed, which in my opinion can often be a choice because we can silence some things on our phones, put them on "do not disturb", or silence or turn off our phones completely. Furthermore, this study showed that high accessibility stress was linked to general stress, sleep disturbances, and depression symptoms. [2] This, in turn, means that letting go of the pressures you put on yourself to always be available to respond quickly could improve your mental health. Additionally, simply spending less time on your phone could also improve your mental health. I highly recommend putting these learnings into practice. Instead of using your phone all the time, try to engage with the world and the people around you. Try to have real human connections.

The pandemic has made many people feel lonely. The most extreme form of loneliness could be living alone during the lockdown, and others suffered from being locked in with the people they were locked in with. The pandemic has highlighted the issues in relationships and has forced many out of relationships. It has also caused struggles and stresses because of too much together time. We need alone time. However, we do not need to feel lonely. If we never have time alone, we will not have time to meditate, plan, journal, be creative, and be productive. Our alone time and the amount we love ourselves is equally as important as the time and love we give others. They are both essential to being happy and feeling fulfilled with life.

We can learn from other people. Once we understand that we are equals with everyone, we will also understand that we can learn from each other. Grandparents can learn from their grandchildren, and friends can learn from friends. It does not matter who is younger and who is older. We can all teach each other something. This is one of the reasons I wrote this book. I wanted to see if people could connect to the things I wrote, and I hope that you will learn something from reading this book.

I love to learn, and I love to share my ideas. I like when people learn things from each other, and it feels nice when people learn things from me. I think we learn something from every person we meet. Other humans teach us how to behave as humans. We see how other people act, how they treat others, and how they treat us. We also learn from each other, as if we all become teachers with the more wisdom and knowledge that we obtain. In the interview I did with my dad and the interview I did with my brother, they both told me that one of their mantras is to learn something from everyone they meet.

My mom and I discussed how my dad and brother display this. I cannot remember my dad ever saying this mantra, but I know he embraces it. He learns from people. He lets them teach him and then adds his own twist to it. When he has a challenge, he problem solves and uses his own knowledge. Once he is in charge of the process, he expands on it. He is willing to volunteer with any swim team I am part of. He learned this from his parents. He helped my club teams, my middle school team, and my high school team. He said, "I wanted the kids to be able to swim and compete. It was always for you and John but also for all the kids." Helping people is a way to learn about and from people.

My brother learns by observing. John approaches things with awe, which he learned from our Papa, my mom's dad. He has the ability to see something done just one time and to learn it from just that. John not only learns quickly, but he also remembers well. One of the people who was instrumental to his growth since he was just a few months old was our Papa. Papa taught all his grandkids about going out of their way to do nice things for people. There is an example of this that will always stay with me, and it is that my grandfather used to offer water to every person who came to collect the trash. They would sometimes decline and sometimes accept, and the ones to accept seemed very relieved to have the water.

A key to my approach as well is that I want to learn for the rest of my life. I want to grow for the rest of my life, and I think a lot of growth comes from learning. I want to grow in many ways, and I have many different ideas for different chapters of my life since that is how I picture my map of life. We each have the power of writing our own stories and making our own choices in life. We get to decide what we do with each day; we decide how we will treat others, and we decide how we will treat ourselves. We control if this talk and self-talk are negative or positive, and if we will be nice to others and ourselves. We cannot control life, but we can control many things in our life, and we can control how we react to the things that happen to us in our lives. People learn from other people.

I think we can learn a lot about each other through sharing different forms of art. One of the easiest forms of art we can share with each other is music. Nowadays, music is so easily accessible with online streaming services. Music can create an experience when it is performed. Music can take us back to a different time and place in our minds or make us think of a certain person. It is one of the single most incredible parts of the human experience. It is difficult to even imagine a world without it. Music makes us feel emotions and it can make us connect deeply with others. There is something so special about finding someone who has a similar taste in music as you and being able to share your music and get recommendations for new music. Sharing art is a way to connect with other people.

I have connected more deeply with the friends I share music with and who share music with me, as I feel we learn a lot about each other that way. A beautiful way to let someone know you are thinking of them is to send them a song you think they would like. Understanding someone else's music taste is a special kind of connection. Having the same music taste as someone else can connect you very deeply, as can other types of art.

Another form of art we can share is books. Book recommendations from your friends or people who interest you can be incredible. This can also lead to great discussions between you and the person who recommended the book since books can be very compelling to discuss. People with different personalities, backgrounds, and lives can come together through books. Reading the stories of others and learning about the experience that others are having in this life is intriguing. I also believe that storytelling is powerful. People have told stories since the start of spoken language. Stories are shared through art. Art is shared by people.

I think that we sometimes have moments that make us feel a real human connection. One of those moments happened to me in 2020 with my friend Maddie, who I wrote about in the Mantras chapter. When I came back from the hospital after days, Maddie and I went for a walk. We talked about what had happened and what it was like for her and what it was like for me. Maddie was in the apartment when the police came during my manic episode. She saw it all happen, and she was still my friend afterward. She could see me beyond what happened to me because she knew me for who I was.

I believe in spreading music, art, books, and movies through word of mouth and sharing the things you like with your friends. I think that there are moments we feel with others when we realize we truly connect with them. We need love to be able to grow, and to have love we need real human connections. We can find inspiration from other people and their stories. We can put our phones down and focus on the people who are sitting right in front of us. The love we give ourselves is just as important as the love we give others. We need each other.

RELIGION OF THE EARTH

TRIGGER WARNING: Psychosis

I believe that the Earth is a god, and more specifically, she is a god. I believe the Earth is a woman. She is commonly known as Mother Earth. She is generous to those who live in harmony with her. She gives to all beings who she carries. She supplies water and food, and she is beautiful. When we are nice to the Earth, when we plant trees and seeds and listen to what the plants and animals are telling us without needing words, we can feel her love the most. I believe that the Earth is a goddess and should be treated as such.

I consider myself to be very spiritual. People who are spiritual but do not belong to a specific religion have many similarities to those who do have a specific religion. One of the similarities is that spiritual and religious people share devotion. Both understand that a person can put time and energy and devote oneself to something and in return will feel better and more fulfilled. As many of those who practice religions find peace in praying to God, I find peace in spending time among the trees and in taking care of plants.

When I was 14 years old, my mom bought me a gift card to go to 10 classes at the local yoga studio and she gave it to me as a Christmas gift. From this, I learned about my spirituality. I loved the ideas that I learned from yoga, such as setting intentions. I learned about mantras. In those first 10 classes, I was fully engaged and present. I learned that focusing on my breath was a strength I possessed. I was not very flexible, but I was figuring it all out and getting better. What I especially loved about yoga was the ending of the classes. I learned about meditating from savasana, the final resting pose on the back. When we would lay on our backs at the end of class and just breathe, the yoga instructors would often turn on some very pleasing music and light an incense, and I would lay there and fully meditate, slowly forgetting about everything and just focusing on my breathing.

I later learned more about meditating. I learned from a therapist while I had psychosis that meditating strengthens your frontal cortex in your brain and makes you more capable of handling stress and panic. I also learned that you can strengthen it a lot before the age of 25. I began to try to put meditating into my routine after he told me this. What I learned was that sitting cross-legged and staring at your wall or your eyelids does not always do the trick. Meditating is not just that, it is so much more. I have learned how helpful it is to meditate with a mantra. I explain more about meditating in the Meditations chapter.

I want to share what spirituality means to me. For a while now I have felt like the main god, or the center of my universe, is the Earth. I can see the Earth. I can touch the Earth. She is more real to me than any other god. "La Tierra" is the word for the Earth in Spanish, and I think that it is incredible that we live on this amazing planet. This planet has mountains, oceans, and forests. Because this planet where we live has such remarkable things,

I believe that we need to try very hard to take good care of her. Taking care of Mother Earth is our responsibility. I find it interesting that the Earth is "la Tierra" in Spanish and that it is also called Mother Earth in English, which means that these two different languages talk about this planet in a feminine way.

People forget that we are guests on this planet. Everything we are given from the Earth is a gift and it should be treated as such. This planet is so large and inhabits millions of living beings. Each living being only has a finite amount of time here. We are guests here, being hosted by Mother Earth. In this life, we get to experience beauty and joy. On this planet, we can see flowers bloom, we can see trees change colors, and we can feel the magic of a forest filled with trees and livelihood. We get to see the sun rise every morning and watch it set every night. We are surrounded by so much beauty every single day just by simply existing here, on this earth, among the magic that she offers.

Ever since learning what it is, I have been intrigued by Taoism. Taoism is both a religion and a philosophy. In Taoism, there is no supreme God. Taoism is about going with the flow or going along with the Tao. The Tao is a cosmic force that flows through all things. Tao means "the way" and it is the principle underlying the universe. It ensures harmony and natural order. Taoism is based on observations of the natural world and the things of the Earth. The creator, Lao-Tzu, wrote a book called the Tao-Te-Ching, which means "The Book of the Way". It is argued that Lao-Tzu may not have been the author of the book, but even if Lao-Tzu was not, it is still a fundamental book in understanding Taoism. [3] The book contains poetry about how people could live more peacefully if they were more mindful of how they impact themselves, others, and the Earth.

There is an idea called destiny. I think the idea of destiny goes along with the idea of the Tao that we should go with the flow of everything. If we have destinies, we will get to them eventually if we always go with the flow and follow what we feel is right or what is calling us. Destiny is about a hidden power that controls the future, which makes me think of how people say that their God has a plan for them. It also makes me think that we should go with the flow and see where it takes us.

The idea of destiny also goes along with something I learned from Concepción Arenal, which is that we should not force anything too much. She wrote about this in the context of professions, and that we should follow the path we feel we should follow without forcing it much. It is the idea that we should let everything flow in a sense, and essentially just go with the flow. I read into this more and think that if we are letting everything flow, we should also be doing the things we want to be doing. We should do what we want for the most part, but we must never forget the pursuit of happiness, which is the right to do what makes you happy if you are not violating the rights of others. We should do what makes us happy often, and we should do the things we want to do. We are writing our own stories, so we can choose a lot of our own future. We cannot control it all and we cannot control our natural talents and interests. Some of it is destiny, and I do not think we should fight with destiny.

Another religion that I am drawn to is Buddhism. I am drawn to it because Buddhist beliefs are similar to my beliefs. In Buddhism, the Noble Eightfold Path is a summary of practices that can lead to liberation. A goal of Buddhism is to reach nirvana, which means that there will be no more suffering. Through nirvana, one can reach liberation from samsara, or the indefinitely repeated cycles of birth, misery, and death. The Noble Eightfold Path lays out that one should strive to have the right understanding, thought, speech, action, livelihood, effort, mindfulness, and concentration. [4]

The eight parts to the path can help with ethical conduct, or sila, mental discipline, or samadhi, and wisdom, or panna. Although I think all parts are beautiful, the part I relate to the most is sila, meaning ethical conduct. Sila is about having universal love for all living beings. We can all practice the religion and spirituality of love.

I meditated very deeply at a Buddhist temple near St. Louis. I had to go somewhere to practice a religion other than any I have ever practiced for a diversity class. I decided I wanted to see what it was like at a Buddhist temple. When I got there, I had to take off my shoes and they taught me how I should sit during meditation. We all sat in silence for about 20 minutes, and then the monk spoke for a while. I was so interested in what he had to say, and I was so deep into meditation that it felt almost as if the world was vibrating.

Lastly, I am attracted to the religion of the Mayans. The Mayan religion is polytheistic, meaning there are many gods. The gods are associated with aspects of nature. Some of the gods are the gods of water, thunder, the sky, agriculture and prosperity, corn, sun, and rain. There is also a god of fertility, a god of thought and intellect, and a nature goddess who protects wild animals. [5] I am drawn to this religion because its center is the Earth. It is also about the sky and everything that goes on around us.

The Mayans were very intelligent. Two thousand years ago, they created their own language, spoken and written, and they invented the mathematical concept of zero. They were excellent at math and knew a lot about astronomy. With this knowledge, they also developed their own calendar. They were also amazing at art, pottery, and architecture. The Mayans lived in an area called Mesoamerica. The civilization started in Yucatan around 2600 B.C. in the land that is now southern Mexico, Guatemala, northern Belize, and western Honduras. The first Mayans were excellent farmers, and they grew corn, beans, squash, and cassava. They also built pyramids. The first complex civilization in Mesoamerica was called the Olmec, and the ideas and culture from the Olmec are present in later civilizations in this area.

A few years ago, I went to Mexico City with my brother, and we took a trip to the pyramids of Teotihuacan, a city that existed in Mesoamerica. The builders of the city remain a mystery to this day. It was believed at one point that the Toltecs built the city, but it was later learned that the pyramids of Teotihuacan existed before the Toltecs. It became a thriving metropolis in

Mesoamerica where people from different cultures came together and formed one of the largest ancient cities in world history. Teotihuacan is a place that feels extraordinary and magical, and it is located less than 30 miles from Mexico City, a place that is even more populated than New York City. [6]

In Teotihuacan, the most important deity was a female. The deity was a Spider Goddess and a creator. The Spider Goddess reminds me of Spider Woman from the stories of the Navajo. Spider Woman was not a creator, but she was a helper and hero. The Spider Goddess appears in art with fangs, jewelry, and vines growing out of her head. Another important goddess at Teotihuacan was the Water Goddess. Great importance was given to the goddesses. [6]

The two great temples of Teotihuacan were named after the sun and the moon. The city has a grid layout and there is a main road called the Avenue of the Dead. At the northern end of the Avenue of the Dead, the second-largest pyramid, the Pyramid of the Moon, stands at 140 feet. South of this pyramid, but not at the southernmost end of the main road stands the Pyramid of the Sun, the largest pyramid in the city. The Pyramid of the Sun is 216 feet tall. [6]

What I find interesting about the larger pyramid being the Pyramid of the Sun is the difference between the sun and the moon. There are different pronouns in the Spanish language for these two words. "La luna" means the moon, and "el sol" means the sun. The sun seems to be thought of as more important than the moon, as it is associated with light and a larger pyramid. The moon is associated with darkness. I believe that the moon is just as important and beautiful as the sun. I think it is interesting that the moon has a feminine pronoun whereas the sun has a masculine pronoun in Spanish. Have you ever noticed that you can often see the moon all day? And that you can also see the reflection of the sun on the moon all night? The moon is closer to the Earth than the sun is, and there is beauty in that alone. The moon is a symbol of femininity. Moons have different phases and a specific time it takes to finish each cycle, and this controls the tides, rains, and seasons.

Right before the sky turns black and the sun sets into a place that we can no longer see from our location on Earth, and when the sun goes down, the moon is much more visible. It is interesting, though, that we are always seeing the sun in some way since the moon reflects the sun's light. The stars also reflect the sun's light. As I wrote before, the stars and the moon have feminine titles in Spanish, whereas the sun has a masculine title. Too much sunlight can damage our skin, and it can even cause cancer. Toxic or overpowering masculinity is like a bad sunburn. It is too harsh, too angry, and too violent. Too much masculinity, like too much sun, can be damaging. On the other hand, the stars and the moon only reflect the sun's light. They show themselves so beautifully in the night sky, shining when there is nothing but artificial light otherwise. Sometimes the moon and the stars shine so brightly, but they do not hurt us. Unlike the sun, we can stare directly in the direction of the moon and the stars.

I think that the sun and the moon are equally important, just like masculinity and femininity. Even though we are always seeing the sun in some way, we are often seeing the moon in some way, too. In fact, the moon is visible in daylight almost every day, but there are times when the moon is not visible during the day. Even if we do not see the moon during the day, we see it at night, and it is illuminated and beautiful every night. There are so many incredible things about the night sky, the moon, and the stars, and we would not be able to see these beautiful things if not for the sun.

After writing about the femininity of the moon, I want to also highlight the femininity of the Earth. I believe that God could be a woman just as much as I believe God could be a man, but I believe She is a woman. I believe this as the pronoun for the Earth in Spanish is "la", and I believe that the Earth is a god and possibly is the main God. Why is it that the Bible describes God as "He"? Why is He the Father? I have questioned that for a long time, and I just do not see why God could not be described as "She". Why does the Bible always refer to God as "He" if no one has ever seen this specific one? God could be male or female, or maybe even a blend of both.

We use a capital E when talking about Earth as a celestial body. Because She is a celestial body, She is some kind of body, and the Earth often shows us that She is a body. She is living in just the same way we are living, too. She needs to see the sun just like us. Mother Earth shares many things with us, such as water and food. She grows food herself so that we will not run out. If we do our part and take care of her properly, She will be able to give back to us as long as the Earth is not inhabited by too many people.

When discussing religion and spirituality, I cannot skip over my ideas about the afterlife. The idea of heaven is something that intrigues me deeply. I think that we are a soul, and we occupy a body. Our souls are essentially inhabiting the body we are in, and this body is a home for our souls. When we treat our bodies nicely, we feel more comfortable in them. This helps our soul, too. I wonder what bodies we would have if we were in heaven. Would we have the bodies that we are in, and would these bodies be in their healthiest and most able state? Would we get a new body in heaven? There are so many different ideas about the afterlife, and just as I do not know which gods I believe in other than the Earth, I do not have a full belief about the afterlife.

What happens after this life with our souls? What becomes of them? Our bodies remain, so maybe our souls do too. I enjoy this way of thought, but I also wonder if our bodies might be the only things that stay. The most beautiful idea to me is that we are reborn as something new, keeping parts of ourselves in each life. Maybe we come back more loving, kinder, and happier each time we are reborn. I am compelled, also, by the idea that we have known someone in a past life, and that is why we can so easily connect with them. This makes me wonder if the thing that happens after death really is rebirth. What if we are reborn as trees, plants, and animals? What if they are the ones that represent us best? I would hope to be a cherry blossom tree, a dog, or a sunflower. What if how we act and treat people in this life really does determine our next step?

Some religions believe that the main problem is that you were born, but others see this life as a miracle. In Buddhism, the goal is to reach nirvana and escape the endless cycle of birth, suffering, and death. In the city of Teotihuacan, the goal was to reach a higher status and to complete the training as a student. When a student would transform into a master at Teotihuacan, and when they would let go of all the boundaries of domestication, they would climb the Pyramid of the Sun and become one with the light. At that moment, they will have completed their training and will become the divine expression of Love or Spirit. [7]

It seems that in many religions, the goal is to reach something other than where we are. We must remember that we are here, and what a wonder it is that we are. We can learn to live in the moment. To simply be. To truly live. To feel the ground beneath us. I see life as a miracle. I see it as a miracle that we get to live among the flowers, the trees, the oceans, the mountains, and all this brilliance and beauty.

FEMININITY, TOXIC MASCULINITY, & THE NEGATIVE CONNOTATIONS OF FEMINISM

TRIGGER WARNING: Narcissism, suicide, toxic masculinity

There are many negative connotations belonging to the word "feminism." Feminism at its core is the movement for equal rights for women. There is also a more specific form of feminism, which is intersectional feminism. Intersectional feminism offers a more detailed description of feminism. It is the advocacy for women having equal rights, no matter their skin color, sexuality, economic status, nationality, religion, or language. I sometimes find that by identifying as a feminist I receive strange looks, and I think people fear calling themselves a feminist. Some people think the word "feminist" has a negative connotation and think that it involves the hatred of men. Others might think that it is the idea that women are better than men. Feminism in its true form, however, is simply about a positive thing, which is equality. It is not about being better than anyone else; feminism is about equality. Something that does not have that same negative connotation is femininity.

A friend explained to me that feminism is sometimes portrayed as women taking on character traits that are inherent to men, such as dominance, aggressiveness, and assertiveness. These traits, especially in a high amount, can be negative. My friend also explains that feminists might act mean because they think that being a feminist means that one must act more masculine. Being mean does not make a person more powerful. Good people and good leaders are nice to others. The world simply does not need more people who display toxic masculinity, who are self-absorbed, and who are abusive.

I asked another friend what he thought feminism was, and he told me that he thought it meant taking pride in female culture. After I told him that feminism was the simple belief that women are equal to men, I asked him if he considers himself to be a feminist. He told me that by this definition, he definitely is a feminist. He believes in equality, and he thinks that women should be leaders because they are capable.

We all must learn to highlight, not hide, our feminine traits, and this goes for men as well. Men can be feminine, just as women can be masculine. The words men and women are not the same as masculine and feminine. Young girls and boys are often taught that they should fit in with one side, and that the side they fit in with should be the sex that they were born as. Sex is different than gender. Sex is not definitively two-sided, as there are intersex people who are born with biological characteristics of both sexes. Furthermore, a person's sex does not have to align with them being more masculine or feminine. People do not have to be completely feminine or completely masculine, and they do not have to identify their gender as male or female, either. There is always something in between. There are issues with thinking in black and white, which leads people to think things are "wrong" because of made-up constructs they have learned from society. Gender is lavender. What I mean by saying gender is lavender is that gender can be between black and white.

An article from Planned Parenthood explains gender identity, what it means to be intersex, and stereotypical gender roles. It is associated with femininity to be polite, accommodating, nurturing, and emotional. On the other hand, being strong, aggressive, bold, and self-confident is associated with masculinity. The article also explains hyper-femininity and hyper-masculinity, which are the overemphasis of embodying socially accepted feminine or masculine traits. Some of the traits listed that are associated with hyper-femininity include being passive, naïve, soft, and graceful. Traits listed that are associated with hyper-masculinity include being insensitive, ambitious, physically imposing, and demanding. [8]

When seeing all these words, you may think about men who embody the masculine words and women who embody the feminine words. I ask you to also consider men who embody traits associated with femininity and women who embody traits associated with masculinity. Men can personify their natural traits associated with being masculine, such as being bold and strong, while also being polite and nurturing. Think also about where you fit into those words. Do you embody the traits that are often associated with femininity or masculinity? You might have a combination of masculine and feminine traits. Do you tend to be emotional? Do you share your feelings with others?

My brother told me, “Femininity is half of us.” Having femininity inside of you is not something to be afraid of, and it can also be protective. Of the people you have interacted with in the world, about half are men and about half are women, statistically. Part of you is who you interact with, and you become more feminine by interacting with and understanding feminine people. It took sperm and an egg to create us. I believe that femininity and masculinity are within us, and we should not be afraid.

I have noticed that many men do not want to cry or show emotion because they are afraid that it is too feminine to do so. I think there is a correlation between this and the fact that men are afraid to reach out for help, leading them to be over three times more likely than women to commit suicide. Sadly, statistics show that white men accounted for 69.67% of suicide deaths in 2018.[9]

Why do men feel like they need to put on a front? Why are they so afraid to ask for help? I think that much of the issue lies in their fear of being too emotional and their fear that emotion is associated with being too feminine. Men want to show others that they are tough and powerful, but doing so can even cost them their lives. Men sometimes strive too much to show their natural characteristics of being independent and brave. Striving to fit with these characteristics can prevent them to ask for help because they think they can do everything on their own. I believe our society must normalize men having and showing emotions, men having depression, and men needing and asking for help from others. We all need each other. We are like the trees; we are all connected and do better when we work together.

I ask you to consider what contributes to the concept of toxic masculinity. Men live shorter lives than women partly because men take more risks. They doubt themselves less, and this makes them more prone to fatal accidents. Some major causes of men's earlier deaths are accidents, suicide, heart disease, and cirrhosis of the liver. Some behaviors are encouraged and accepted more among men than women, and because these lead to death, they can be viewed as toxic expectations of men. Men act fearless, use more guns, work more hazardous jobs, drink more alcohol, and smoke more than women do. These behaviors tie into toxic masculinity because they are encouraged and accepted among men, leading them to be expected. Nothing is requiring men to partake in these behaviors, but men may feel the societal pressure to do them, just because they are men. When will everyone realize that toxic masculinity hurts everyone, including men? [10, 11]

Toxic masculinity is more than just being risky and fearless. It is also about the overemphasis of the traits used to describe masculinity. Those traits are being bold, self-confident, strong, and aggressive. These can be exaggerated into toxic traits. Being overly bold is associated with taking risks. Being too bold could cause someone to take a risk that has harmful consequences. Self-confidence can be wonderful unless it becomes narcissism. Strength is power; however, it is possible to come off too strong. Coming off too strong is about being overly forceful with others. Being overly aggressive can be toxic, too.

As a feminist writing about equality, I write a lot about the differences between the sexes. The fact of the matter is that men and women have differences. We cannot deny that we have differences in our biology. Sex is different than gender. A person's sex can determine who they compete with in a sport. Even after someone transitions, transgender females might still be required to compete with males. The fact is that men are naturally stronger and can build more muscle. Women can be strong too, but it shows in sports and many other areas that men and women are not born with the same biology.

We are equal, but we are different. We are all individuals with different things to offer to the world. We are more than just female or male or a mixture of the two. We are all human beings. I believe gender is something that is lavender, as I will explain later. Gender is not black and white at all. I believe that men and women can be a mixture of masculine and feminine, and that no one should be ashamed of having characteristics of another gender. In the end, we are all just people. We are all living among the trees, flowers, and animals and we are all human. We are equal.

My cousin, Clara, is a woman who considers herself to be both very masculine and very feminine. She is very emotional, but she is self-confident. She is aggressive and not afraid to speak up about the fact that she wants to be helpful. As a farmer, she had to be aggressive, or she would not get to do things. Clara attended a university where she studied agriculture and agronomy. Afterward, she went on to become a farmer. Clara farmed for years and became the operations manager of a 2,000-acre farm. The farm had anywhere from 1,000 to 1,500 cows. Now, she is working in the medical field as a patient care technician, and this is a stepping-stone for where she really wants to be. Clara saw and experienced farming, an industry dominated by men, before switching to experiencing nursing, an industry dominated by women.

I talked to Clara about what it was like to be a female in a male-dominated occupation. She told me that she felt like she stuck out. Additionally, she did not have many of the skills that most men she worked with learned when they were young. She constantly had to learn new things. When she was trained, she was expected to already know how to do what she was being trained to do. She told me about how she feels that when a man makes a mistake, it is seen as just a mistake. When a woman makes a mistake, it is often seen that she has weaknesses. It might also be used as evidence that someone is not qualified to do what they are trying to do. When women must ask to learn something that the men have known how to do for much of their lives, men often fail to spend enough time teaching the task since it does not seem difficult to them anymore. This occurs frequently in farming since it is an occupation where you must know how to operate many things including heavy machinery, and little boys are taught more about using tools and fixing things than little girls. Because of this societal norm, many women do not feel comfortable fixing cars or doing similar tasks.

Clara listed some of the difficulties of working in the farming industry and a male-dominated industry in general. One of those difficulties is that farming has not embraced all the norms that unions have fought for. It is a very conservative industry and she believes it does not promote self-care. Rather, it is all about hard work and working yourself to the point that you cannot work anymore. It is hard to feel valued and appreciated in this type of atmosphere. People see farming as a lifestyle, not an occupation. It is hard work with little pay and there is the expectation to do dangerous tasks. Another struggle of working in the industry was that she did not feel like she could have kids. She did not know any other women with her job. The job was so stressful and time-consuming that she did not think she could support a child, even if she wanted to.

I wrote earlier in this chapter about my brother and how he talked about how statistically, approximately half of the people we interact with in our lives will be women. We are influenced by the people we meet and interact with. As a farmer, Clara interacted mainly with men. She believes that male-dominated professions could benefit from more women and that female-dominated industries could benefit from more men. When you have an occupation that does not reflect the demographics of a region, it points to something culturally wrong. There needs to be a better representation of minorities. Clara says that there are issues and barriers to entry when the demographics of an occupation do not reflect the demographics of the area. She felt like being a female farmer was a feminist act, but she never really felt like she was inspiring any other women by being one. When women take part in male-dominated occupations, they might take on traits or characteristics they learn from men instead of using their natural traits. Because of this, it will take time for there to be changes in an industry as a whole, even if more women join it. She was not sure she would recommend other women to such a difficult situation. After many years, Clara decided to get a new job.

I asked her why she wanted to go into nursing, and one of the reasons is that she believes that the healthcare industry has embraced taking care of its workers much more than farming has. It also gives her time to farm on her own. She still plans to farm in some way even while she works in the medical field. She told me that she has always felt that she is meant to take care of things. She believes she can have a very big impact on the world by taking care of human beings, so she decided to switch to working in health care. She loves taking care of plants around her house. She likes giving care. She minored in agronomy in school and learned how to take care of plants. Clara also learned a lot about taking care of plants from her mom and our Granny. She learned how to find a baseline and how to notice when things are not at their baseline. It is, she explained, about learning how to correct it or who to contact to correct it. To take care of plants, you must be detail-oriented and caring. To take care of people, you must do the same.

The moon and the stars are said as “la luna” and “las estrellas” in Spanish. These words, along with the word “la Tierra” are all feminine words. All these very special and beautiful things are expressed with femininity. I believe that femininity is the future. I think that women can change the world. Some characteristics of femininity that I see are supportiveness, empathy, kindness, and warmth. Feminine people are known to be nurturing, willing to take care of others, and mainly care deeply about others. In general, women care more for groups, whereas men are more individualistic.

There is an article about the advantages of having women in teams called “Defend Your Research: What Makes a Team Smarter? More Women.”, an article from the Harvard Business Review. [12] The article describes an experiment showing that a group’s collective intelligence has little to do with the individual IQs of its members, but that there is a correlation between the intelligence of the group and having more women in it. In the experiment, two professors randomly assigned people to teams and gave them standard intelligence tests. Based on how they did on these tests as a team, they earned a score. What they found was very interesting. When Malone, one of the authors of this article, was interviewed, they explained that these findings are preliminary, but that so far, the data shows that when there are more women, the group is stronger. Malone agrees that groups of women are smarter than those of men and says that it is explained by the social sensitivity that women have shown. This shows that what is truly important in a group setting is social sensitivity, which can be found in men as well. It is something that comes more naturally to women, but this does not go to say that men cannot be socially sensitive.

I think a lot about the fact that the U.S. has never had a female president. In a little girl's life today, she learns at some point what the name of the president is, and then she learns that all the previous presidents in this country have been men. Because of this, a little girl who might have grown up to try to be the president of the U.S. might decide that she cannot do it since no one woman has ever done the job before. In fact, she can do whatever she wants. No job should be done by only men.

I have always thought about the fact that my age each year, until my birthday in October, is the same as the current year. I was 20 in 2020. My 20th year was one of the most difficult ones yet, and I think that I came back from it much stronger than I was before. In 2020, and while I was 20, I transferred schools, got sent home to Michigan from New Orleans due to the pandemic, ended up in a psychiatric hospital twice, and voted for the first time. One of the most dramatic parts of 2020 was that there was a U.S. presidential election during a global pandemic. There was a rainbow at the end of the year in November, when on the 100th year that women could vote, we elected our first female vice president. I think there is something very special about the 20s, including the 1920s and the 2020s.

Think about the things that a female vice president, or better yet a female president, could bring to this country. Nature suggests that she will be motherly and caring. Now, little girls will learn that their vice president is a woman, and more specifically a BIPOC (Black, Indigenous, People of Color) woman, and they will realize that they belong in places where decisions are being made. Because we elected a woman to be vice president, a little girl may aspire to be vice president or president. She will learn that she can stand up for herself and she can be powerful. She will realize that she can do anything.

When I first read the article "¿Qué Oficios y Profesiones Pueden Ejercer Las Mujeres?" which translates to "What Trades and Professions Can Women Practice?" [13] I was skeptical because of its title. I thought to myself, "Women and men can do the same professions." As I read into it more, and I read more about the author, Concepción Arenal, I learned that she was the original Spanish feminist of the 1800s. She is called the "pioneer of Spanish feminism" and was the founder of the feminist movement in her country. She was the first woman to attend university in Spain and she specialized in law, journalism, and poetry. I learned that I agreed with her on a lot more than I originally thought I would when I read the title of her article. Arenal believed that women needed to contribute to politics. They were not able to in her time. She also believed that the main inequality between men and women and their potential lies in their education.

Another topic that Arenal wrote about was the lack of involvement of women in politics. Arenal believed that women are intelligent. She believed that they should have opinions and influences on politics in the 1800s before women even had the right to vote in Spain. Today, we still see a lack of women in politics. I previously wrote about how we still have yet to have a female president in the U.S., and it makes me wonder about some things. Are women afraid for their voices to be heard? Where are they still being held back? When will we finally see a female become president in this country?

My friend, JeAnnah, talks about how she wants to get more education, and potentially keep going to school until she gets a Ph.D. JeAnnah recently finished her undergraduate degree in psychology, and she works with kids who have autism. She already went to chef school and is a certified chef, but she realized that she wanted to get a degree and study psychology to be able to contribute more to her job. The company she works for belongs to her mom, who created a business when JeAnnah almost lost her life from chickenpox complications. Doctors did not even know if JeAnnah would survive, and at one point she was paralyzed. She suffered brain damage. Her mom searched for any type of therapy or treatment for her daughter that existed. They tried so many things and found hyperbaric oxygen treatment, and it worked like a miracle for JeAnnah. Slowly but surely, she began to recover. Miraculously, you would never be able to tell that JeAnnah went through this as a child if you just met her. She is smart, fun, and easy to talk to.

Because the hyperbaric oxygen treatment did so much good for JeAnnah's family, her mom decided to start her own business with this treatment. It is now a very established business. Her mom also created a foundation that raises money for families that cannot afford treatments for their children. Her mom has multiple leadership awards. Naturally, JeAnnah looks up to her mom and is attracted to the same amount of success that she has. JeAnnah told me about how impactful it is that her mom has a Ph.D. with being an entrepreneur of a company that offers a form of healthcare. Since she has a Ph.D., people understand that she has a wealth of knowledge, and they are more likely to trust her. Great leaders are trusted by people. Educated women are powerful.

Because men and women have not always been equal and historically did not get equal education, women are held back. Arenal believed that the fundamental difference in the inequality of men and women is education. Women are not inferior intellectually. Being the first woman in her country to go to college, Arenal saw that other women had the power to do what she was doing, and that they were intellectually capable of attending university and doing the same jobs as men. She did argue, however, that women are more compassionate, sensitive, and moral than men are, leading them to be more capable of doing some jobs better than men naturally can.

Arenal argued that we should leave some jobs to men and some to women, and that the jobs that would be done better by women should be done by them. This part of her article discusses the idea that men and women may be naturally made for different jobs and should do what they have a comparative advantage in. This will create a better society. I want to take this idea even further than Concepción Arenal did. I want to argue that women are natural leaders. I have written more about this in the chapter called Leading with a Feminine Approach. Something to notice is that women, compared to men, more often garden, care about nature, know how to be caregivers, and take care of animals.

A truth is that many women are capable of bearing children. Because many women can birth children, they are naturally more caring, nurturing, and motherly. In a traditional family structure with a mother and a father, moms in the family are often the main caregivers, and also the parent who makes many of the decisions. Many mothers make the rules but also give emotional support when someone in the family needs it. Some children are raised by a single parent, and some are raised by those who are part of the LGBTQ community, and the role of the decision-making parent differs. Men can perform the traditional or societally accepted role of a mother by caring for the children and the emotional needs of the family. I think that some men might be a better fit to perform the role of the caregiver. In my eyes, the caregiver is the true leader of a family. The breadwinner may be the one who supports the family the most financially, but this is often because the caregiver has a much more time-consuming and emotionally tiring job with the family. My own upbringing was very traditional in that I was raised by my own biological mom and dad, so certainly this impacts my vantage point.

Arenal believed that women were not born to command by force. She believed that women dominate by persuasion and affection. Coercion, the use of force or threats to persuade others, is not naturally feminine. Arenal believed that women should stay away from coercion. I do not think that women were made to be the police that we have today. Furthermore, female police officers in general should not attempt to be more like the male officers, but instead they should let their feminine or motherly traits shine. Men struggle more with sharing their emotions, and in turn, can seem to be emotionless. I believe there must be some correlation between a lack of empathy and emotions and being willing to kill another human being, as we see happen with some police. Lethal force, or the killing of people by some police, should only be done as a last resort. It should be a priority for police officers to respect the right to life of human beings. I think that they use too much force and not enough emotion. They can appear as if they do not have feelings. I think that the police could benefit from more females and more femininity.

The words and thoughts associated with today's police in the U.S. are not the same words and thoughts associated with femininity. This needs to change. We need police who care, who show emotion, who nurture, who are humble, and who are collaborative with others. We do not need more police, nor do we need more leaders, who are overly forceful, dominant, and aggressive. When I think of the word police, I think of policemen, I think of masculinity, and I think of toxic and poisonous power. Maybe women are not meant to rise to the top of a system that is built on toxic masculinity. Maybe women are not in the highest roles as often as men because the highest roles have been skewed to expect that women will lead like men. We need change. We need reform, new ideas, and more people treating people like plants. Imagine a world where half of police officers are women. Likewise, imagine a world where half of the CEOs, managers, and political leaders are women. Imagine what this world would be like.

The idea from Concepción Arenal is not a rule. Some women were not made to dominate by sweetness, affection, and persuasion, as Arenal believed, but instead can dominate with their fierce self-confidence, boldness, and strength. The second grouping of words are the same words that I previously listed to be associated with masculinity. Some women are more masculine than others, just as some men are more feminine than others. We must not be ashamed of who we are naturally. Instead, we should embrace our innate traits.

I wrote in an essay a few years ago, translated to English, that, "Because of the historical atmosphere in Spain, the women of the XIX century did not have any other option than to transcend their role outside of care and peace. Today, women and men can and should do whatever profession pertains to them. If women are not educated, they can never contribute more to society. Education empowers people, which was exactly what the women in Spain needed to contribute to the advances of society. We have put artificial limits on the well-being of the world." I believe that we have put artificial limits on the well-being of the world because of the glass ceiling, which is an imaginary barrier that limits women from filling top leadership roles, and because of limiting women from having the same education as men.

Once everyone has the same rights and once everyone is seen as an equal, the world will not put limits on people anymore. We will no longer be so impressed when we see a woman in a high leadership role or when she is making great change for the better in the world. We must remember that we are all individual people with different traits and different ideas to offer. We are not our genders; we are all human beings. We should be as feminine or as masculine as we naturally are.

WOMEN HAVE POWER

Women are powerful people. Not only do women have different innate qualities than men, lending them to be great leaders, but women may have the power to give birth to another human being. Many women reproduce and bring new people into the world. In religions, there are so many different creation stories to explain mankind. Similarly, every single human comes with a creation story. All humans are birthed by someone with a uterus. Most people on this planet have a mother who birthed them, and we all share the same mother called Earth. We endearingly call her Mother Earth because she is our mother, too.

Men and women differ in emotional intelligence as well as in the way they express their emotions. I believe women hold power when it comes to emotion because they are more emotionally intelligent and are more expressive of their emotions. [14, 15] Women live longer than men do, suggesting that they are more resilient than men. Additionally, men are much more likely to pass away within the first six months after their spouse passes away. [16] Women are naturally different than men. They are arguably better caregivers by nature. Because of this, women can become people who change the world. They can choose if they want to use their power for good. When they choose to use their power for good, they might become nurses, doctors, authors, caregivers, teachers, mothers of adopted children, influential grandmothers, leaders, or an endless number of other amazing roles.

I talked about the resilience of women with a resilient woman that I know, which is my mom. She has shown resilience and patience throughout my struggles with my mental health. She has also shown resilience throughout my entire life by responding to hardships with optimism and positivity. My mom thinks that women are special when it comes to resilience. She explained that some women can bear children. There is physical resilience after a body goes through all those changes. Having children is not easy. Women go through more physical changes and challenges in their life than men do. As a woman, you continually face challenges that are out of your control. This makes women into strong people. If you can adapt to things well, you are more resilient. Women are not as physically strong as men are, but they are still very strong. Women must adapt to so much. My mom also noted how women are often more emotional and in tune with their feelings, making them respond and react differently to everything. Some men are more resilient than women are, but I believe that women are generally more resilient than men.

Women have power in relationships. Women have power because they can decide to expect more from men or their partners. They can understand that they are so much more than objects and that they should never accept any kind of "love" where a man or partner treats them as so. Part of this power is to realize that we can stop compromising. We can stop expecting less than what we want from others. A power that we can all have is the power to evaluate our relationships. We can realize when a person is not positively adding to our lives, and we do not have to continue a relationship with them if they are not.

Any relationship you have should add to your life, not drag you down. If it is dragging you down, it needs work. A struggling relationship is like a plant. If you see your plant turning brown and it's supposed to be green, it either needs more or less water or sun. It might need a change of soil or a differently sized pot. This is a metaphor for relationships. I mean that when relationships are struggling, we either need to give them more or less attention. This might mean giving someone some space, or it might mean giving them more love and spending more time with them.

On the other hand, it is sometimes past the point of no return meaning it is the end of a relationship. The plant might be dead meaning it no longer needs water or sunlight. Maybe something very bad happened or enough small bad things built up and the relationship is now not as enjoyable as it used to be and not as happy as you want it to be. These feelings are valid. You are able to end relationships that no longer serve you or make you feel good. What you are feeling about and with the people you associate with is so important. It can either make you feel good or bad to spend time with a certain person. Pay attention to this energy because it is not something to ignore.

Women have the power to walk away because they can do so. We should all know our worth and have high standards for other people because of it. It can take time to walk away. People get stuck in abusive and terrible relationships for years and do not feel they have the power to end it, but we all have power. This chapter is about women having power, but we all have power as people. It can be very difficult, but we have the power to walk away from situations that are unhealthy, and we have the power to say no.

Some girls must be taught by a guy how to be treated by a guy. For me, a person named Diego helped set the standard for men. He never made me feel uncomfortable, but instead made me feel more comfortable. I knew I liked Diego from the start. He was easy to get along with, and we always just seemed to have a good time and liked a lot of the same things. He is very smart, and I noticed that quickly. I love to pay for half of the meals because it simply does not make sense to me that one person should always pay, and he would let me pay for half of the meals. Diego suggested great restaurants. The night I realized I liked Diego was the night that we went out downtown with his friends to see his roommate's band perform. I was not feeling well, it was late, and I realized I should not be there when we were arriving downtown. I told Diego I needed to go home, so he ordered an Uber for the two of us. He told me it was too late for me to go alone. I appreciated it because it made me feel safe. Many people understand how it feels to be alone late at night and to feel nervous, scared, and unsafe.

Even though Diego taught me so much, the person who first set the high standard of men was my brother. He taught me to expect respect. John and I began to get along very well when he was in high school. Once he went off to college, and since he was not very far away, we started to get very close. John was the first person with whom I ever tried alcohol. He stressed that he wanted me to learn what my limits were. By doing so, I would be less likely to go past them as I would already know that there are consequences and that self-control could protect me from being taken advantage of. Because of these men who made my standard higher, I do not appreciate toxic masculinity. I have learned how to expect more from men by learning from men.

I also experience being treated with respect from Kris, who has taught me so much about happy and healthy relationships. He is a great example of someone who gives the level of respect I should expect. Kris understands emotional boundaries, and he respects them. In general, he has a lot of respect. Kris does so much for the people he cares about. He knows how to solve problems. I look for this in people because my dad and my Papa exemplified these qualities to me.

During my sophomore year of college, I learned how to be independent. I lived in a single dorm room, and it was my first time living alone. I had never before been so motivated and driven in my entire life. When the spring came along and the flowers started to bloom, I also learned to be happy being single for the first time. I was not looking for a relationship with anyone other than my friends, and I felt so happy and free. As one of my mantras says, we are not halves. We need to recognize that as women, we do not need another person or half to make us whole. We also do not have to have children. We might be taught that we need to have a significant other and that we need to get married, but we have the power to make choices. We have the capability as women to be powerful and strong on our own if we choose to do so. We are writing the stories of our lives, and we are capable and welcome to live them as independently as we please.

The fact that women live longer than men shows that they are powerful. I think this is because women live longer than men due to biological, behavioral, and environmental factors. Women, on average, live six to eight years longer than men, varying depending on where they live. Newborn girls are more likely to live until their first birthday than newborn boys. Some biological differences of women are that they have less fat surrounding their organs than men do. Women tend to have more fat directly under their skin. The fat surrounding men's organs causes them to be more likely to develop cardiovascular diseases, something that contributes to the lower longevity of men. [17] If we see this life as a blessing, longevity is power.

Because of a small biological difference, women have the power of developing fewer cardiovascular diseases than men, and in turn, have longer life expectancies. Women have other powers, too. Women can use the power that they have to make the world a better place. We all have the power to expect happiness and goodness from the relationships that we share with others. If someone does not add to your life, you can ask yourself if that person should still be a part of it. We can decide that enough is simply enough. Women live longer, are incredibly resilient, and they also have the powers that their natural traits give them. Women must simply decide to use these powers to their fullest and let the bright light inside of them radiate.

FEELING BIG AND SMALL

There is an idea of feeling big and small. To me, this is about how we are each writing our own stories that belong to nobody else but ourselves. We get to write our own because we get to make our own choices. Our choices determine our lives. Our level of education determines to an extent what our life will be like. For example, I think that a person with a Ph.D. has a much higher likelihood of having a fulfilling life than a person who does not know how to read. Unfortunately, many people do not have access to quality education. This does not mean that they will be unhappy, but it might make their lives more difficult than the people who have access to education. We did not choose where we are from, how much money our family had when we were born, the tone of our skin, and many other things. We can, in fact, choose if we will approach things optimistically or pessimistically, and likewise, we can control how we react to things. We may be able to make choices about where we want to live, what we want to do for work, and what we want to do for fun. If we are fortunate, we are able to choose how much education to achieve. We do not get to write our entire story on our own, since some of it gets written for us, as that is how life is, but we do get to decide much of our stories.

I realized at a young age how amazing it felt to stand and look out at an ocean, something so grand and big and beautiful, and to feel so small. The song "Good Life" by Zhu has become important to me. Its lyrics make me truly feel something about being big and small. These lyrics are about how your life can simultaneously be your own story as well as everyone else's story. In the introduction of the song, there is a question asked that reminds me that I am both big and small. This question is a fascinating one. How can you see things from your own vantage point, and at the same time also consume yourself with actually living your experiences? If life is all about our own stories, we are big, we are almighty, we are powerful. If life is not about us as individuals, we are tiny and insignificant. We are all of these at the same time.

You are writing your own story. In this story, you are the main character. You are the center of the whole thing. You are fundamental and essential, and without you, there would be no story. In the real world, outside of your story, are millions of other stories. Yours is just a tiny piece. However, your story is the only one that you know in its entirety, and the only person you must spend the rest of your life with is you.

There are places that give me the feeling of being big and small. For me, a place that I feel very small is when I am looking at the ocean or a very big lake. I also feel very small when I am on a mountain, and when I am at the very top of the mountain, I feel a different sensation too, and it is a combination of feeling big and small at the same time. I feel big and small at the pool, too. When I stand in front of a pool, I feel big. Once I dive into the water, I begin to get lost in it, and I start to feel smaller. The whole experience I have while I am swimming seems like a whole different world. I feel small when I look up at the night sky. I realize how far away everything is in this galaxy, and how far away the moon is, even though it is relatively close compared to everything else.

I feel small when I go to a place that I never have been, and I feel small when I go to a place that I only visit for short times. I feel big when I am home or in a city that I have lived in, as it feels like I know so much more about what is going on around me. When we are home, we get to make so many decisions and we are very powerful. We all have these significant places, the places that make us feel big, and they are different for people all around the world.

I feel very small when I pass by and see other people living lives that I know nothing about. I feel small when I drive or walk by a window showing people eating together. When this happens near home, I think about how that person lives in a similar location as me but has a completely different life than I have. These moments make me feel like my life is running in a parallel with other lives around me, and they make me realize how many people there are that I do not know. It is an exciting thought to think that there are so many people who we have not met yet that we could love so much. It is an odd feeling that there are so many other human beings alive on this earth while we are.

In the Meditations chapter, I write about mindfulness meditation. Mindfulness means that you must pay attention to what is going on around you, as that is a part of awareness. This also reminds me of the song I referenced earlier by Zhu. An amazing way to live is to be present and in the moment, while also being able to reflect on your life. When we think about everyone in the world, it is easy to feel small and insignificant, but we must never forget that we are essential to our own stories and the stories of those close to us.

The final subject that I want to bring up about feeling big and small at the same time is popularity. Some things get big, meaning they get popular. Some people become stars from being great musicians, speakers, writers, sports players, and other things. When something becomes the most popular, it obviously becomes the most well-known too. There is a reason why Rupi Kaur is such a popular poet, why so many people know raps by Drake, and why Michael Phelps is such a widely known swimmer. It is because these people are stars of their crafts. They are the best of the best. They are the biggest, but in the end, they are just people. They are small at the same time.

We create so much of our lives. The strangers that you pass have stories, relatives, friends, hobbies, interests, and knowledge just like you do. They, too, sometimes feel big and sometimes feel small. People can feel irrelevant and insignificant sometimes, but we can all remember that we can do something big by being on this earth. We can make this world better with our existence. We are big and small at the same time.

GROWING FOR THE REST OF MY LIFE

TRIGGER WARNING: Sexual assault, psychosis, mania, suicide, schizophrenia

Sometimes, we feel stuck. We feel like we will always feel as terrible as we feel. We then, like many times, have some options. We can either give up, or we can come back from it. Coming back from hardships and struggles is always the best option. Healing with some ease is called resilience. In our lives, we are always learning. We are always growing into more mature and knowledgeable versions of ourselves. We can make those selves resilient and strong by learning to grow through what we go through.

I have a tattoo to symbolize a very important mantra for me, which is growth. In addition to loving the symbolism I have linked to ivy, I have also always loved what ivy looks like, whether it is on the side of a house, in the form of jewelry, or drawn. The tattoo I have is a symbol to grow through tough situations because ivy does that. Ivy is a plant that is known to grow and even thrives in harsh conditions. I strive to be like ivy. This ivy tattoo will be part of me and go with me forever. I will see it every day for the rest of my life, and this is a good thing because I like to set intentions. I love the repetition of mantras. Because of this, I decided that the underlying intention for the rest of my life will be growing. Becoming wiser. Becoming more independent. Seeking intrinsically for validation and not from others. Becoming a better human being. Growing.

I grew a lot in 2020. I was changed by 2020. It changed people's lives, including mine. The year slowed me down, it gave me lots of time to think, and it taught me about myself. I learned about what and who I truly care about. The year drew a thick black line between love and hate. It created division but it also created some unity, or lavender. I learned to be grateful for my health when I have it, and it has brought me to care about the health of others, my community, and my world more than ever before. The year 2020 taught me patience as well as solitude. It taught me that I can be positive and optimistic even if my world seems like it is falling apart. I also learned not to hide my emotions and feelings because doing that has previously not worked for me. I think I came out of 2020 stronger than I was before.

It will take us a long time to forget about all of this. In fact, 2020 will be written about in textbooks. Little kids will ask their grandparents about it. I have always thought there was something special about the fact that I was as old as the number of years past the year 2000. The year 2020 was the year I turned 21. If I were to read a book about my future at a younger age, I would read that in 2020 there would be a global pandemic and that it would completely change everything. I would read that 2020 would be the most difficult year I would have and that I would be going to the psychiatric hospital twice in the same year. I would learn that it would feel like my world is crashing and burning sometimes. I would also read that I would learn so much about myself in 2020 and that I would become closer to being the fullest and best version of myself.

We have many choices that we make in our lives. One of the main things we decide regularly, often subconsciously, is how we react to what happens. We can take our struggles, our trauma, and our hardships and we can allow them to consume us and dictate our lives, or we can take them and learn to run with them and continue living on. We can decide to still enjoy this life, even when bad things happen. We can learn to dance with our demons. We do not control life, but we do control how we react to it.

We had the choice to use the tough year of 2020 to take out our stress and frustrations on others, or we could understand that the year was rough for those around us, too. Because of this, we needed to show more kindness and love than ever before. Something that we learn throughout life is to develop and make changes for the sake of those we love. Adapting to the needs of others and adapting to the new needs of ourselves is growth. To adapt, we must change the ways that we have always done things and turn them into something new.

We can use trauma and negativity in our lives to help us grow and learn about ourselves. First, we must heal. Second, we must grow, just like the trees and the flowers do. A tree that I did not want was planted in me in 2018. I kept trying to cut down the poisonous tree without getting to the roots of it.

I repeatedly tried to ignore it, so I tried planting sunflower seeds on top, but the poisonous tree kept growing and resurfacing. In 2020, when I stopped caring for my sunflowers enough, the poisonous tree started to grow, take over the sunflowers, and hurt me. The poisonous tree was the sexual assault that happened to me freshman year. I see this as a leading reason for why I ended up in the hospital for two psychiatric emergencies within a five-month time frame.

We need to get to the roots of our issues, and until we do that, we cannot fully heal. We need to understand what is hurting us and how it makes us feel. We need to get to the roots. After it happened to me, I felt an emptiness inside. I went to only two therapy sessions. I wanted to avoid pain. I acted like everything was fine to my friends and teammates and that I felt okay. I did not tell them that I was nervous that I would see him, even though I had never seen him before what happened, every time I left my room. The first time I thought that I saw him, I had my first panic attack, and I went back to hide away in my room. I remember wanting all the feelings and the flashbacks to just go away, but they did not. I thought that if I acted like everything was fine, and if I just ignored and did not talk about what had happened, it would eventually get better. Ultimately, the magic of time began to heal me a bit, but it was simply not enough. We need to let out our concerns and our feelings somehow, and we cannot leave them bottled up inside without facing the consequences of doing so. I later learned that one of the causes of psychosis is trauma. I also learned that untreated mental illnesses, as well as treated ones, can cause psychosis.

In both situations when I ended up in the psychiatric hospital, I had one or more flashbacks to the assault within a day before going to the hospital. This shows that although it may seem like you are healed from something, you might not fully be healed. Healing takes a lot of work, and it takes a lot of patience. I went to the psychiatric ER for the first time in May of 2020, when I had psychosis. When the doctors diagnosed me, I did not even know what the word psychosis meant. Psychosis is a terrifying experience.

During psychosis, a person loses touch with reality, and they may even begin to hallucinate. When a person is mentally ill in this way, they may have delusions and a struggle to function overall. The scariest part of the experience was that the delusions led me to not trusting anyone. I did not trust the nurses, I did not trust the doctors, and worst of all, I did not trust my parents. When I get anxious, I often catastrophize, which means that I assume that the worst is going to happen, often with no evidence to back up this idea. When I had psychosis, and days before my parents took me to the hospital, I had somehow convinced myself that they did not want me in their lives anymore. I convinced myself that they did not want me in their house anymore and that they were both intending to leave me somewhere with no plans to pick me up. I thought they wanted to get rid of me. When they took me to the psychiatric ER, I screamed and cried and held on tightly to my dad's truck because I thought they were dropping me off somewhere with plans to never pick me up.

When I had psychosis and left the psychiatric ER after a long day there, I remember feeling an immense joy on the way home. My parents were taking me home, back into their arms and their love, and I was so happy. It was one of the first times I felt trust and love in days. The other time I felt it, and when I knew my mom loved me, was when she held my hand and sang me a lullaby while I was panicking in the hospital.

Before I went to the hospital, I had been going through psychosis for a few days. Prior to everything happening, my mom and I planned to visit my Granny, her mom. I remember being in the car with my parents on the way to take lunch to her. I could barely focus on what anyone was saying. It was the beginning of the pandemic, and I was still very nervous about seeing my Granny because of everything going on. I was afraid of getting her sick, and I was nervous to see her in the state that I was in. When we arrived, I got even more anxious. I was so anxious that I did not want to enter her house, so I stood in the garage staring at nothing and felt as if my feet would not move me into her house, no matter how hard I tried. We left her house because I was acting so strange, and I was filled with the awful feelings of guilt and embarrassment. In my paranoid state, I was not sure if my Granny would ever forgive me for how strange I acted.

I spoke to Carolyn about what it was like for her when I had psychosis. I was stuck in a paranoid state for weeks and she came to help me in the beginning. When she heard about what happened, she came to see me. She told me about how difficult it was that I did not want to go outside. I was afraid my parents would change the locks if I left. She wondered if her friend would ever be the same again. After she could finally get me to leave my house, I would tell my mom where I was going once again by giving her a call, and I would set an alarm for when I had to take my medication.

We talked about how I did not want to take my meds. I thought they might hurt me, and I was scared to take them. She had to convince me every time to take them. She would lift my hand to my mouth with the pill on it, and I would take it. She would make me open my mouth to ensure I swallowed it. There is a stigma behind taking mental health medications. There is also a stigma around going to therapy. It makes people think of weakness. Sometimes, these are the most important things you can do. It is important to get help immediately if you think you need it, and it can be helpful to be open and trusting to those who truly want to help you. Carolyn and I talked about how taking medications makes everything more real. Medications can help prevent issues, and for me, they prevent psychosis and mania. It is very likely for people who experience these illnesses to experience them again.

Every time I would take my medication, Carolyn would say, "Take these, they are good for you." Every morning, my mom would say, "One day at a time." It was these little reminders that got me through it. Their kindness, empathy, love, and care were more than I ever knew I would receive. It was truly incredible. My mom and Carolyn worked together to make sure I was doing the right things and taking the right steps to heal. They both encouraged me to swim, which is one of my favorite ways to think and meditate.

I hated the word "better." Whenever someone would ask if I was getting better, it would really upset me. I did not know if I was getting better because it felt like a roller coaster. One minute I felt fine, then the next I was crying because I thought I heard gunshots. Carolyn could not say the word "better." One time, she told me to take the medications because they would make me feel better, and I got upset. I did not like that word when everything was changing so much from one moment to the next. It was scary to me. I wrote in a journal that I kept while I had psychosis, "I don't think I'll get better."

Carolyn and I spoke about how the best things you can do for your mental health are taking your medications, exercising, meditating, journaling, and going to therapy. When I had psychosis, Carolyn wrote down a list of things I could do to take care of myself. One thing that really helped me was meditating in any form. My favorite meditations are swimming, walking, and cooking.

When I had psychosis, I did not trust my parents and I told them that they were trying to kill me or get rid of me. It took me a while for the words "I love you", when coming from them, to start making sense again. Because my mom is a bit more expressive of her affection and talks more about her feelings and emotions, I was able to comprehend the words from her earlier than I could comprehend them when my dad said them. At the end of the summer, my dad flew with me to help me move into my new apartment in New Orleans, and when left he told me, "I love you; I would do anything for you." I could not stop crying. My brain finally learned to accept his love again. It accepted it truly and fully.

After I quit swimming my sophomore year of college, prior to my psychosis experience, I started to become increasingly anxious. I did not swim at all for about six months. I started swimming for pleasure after those six months, but I did not do it regularly. In the fall, I realized that I really wanted to swim again, but that I did not want to do it at Lindenwood. I wanted a whole new experience, a new school, and a new city. In the fall, I also got depressed. I was not sure what was going on when I could barely get myself out of bed in the morning even though it was 10 am, and I did not understand why my hands were so shaky. I tried going to the school therapist, but it reminded me of when I was there after the assault.

When I have swimming in my life, I do not feel as anxious or depressed. I love starting the day with a swim, and I feel like I can accomplish more with my day and feel more fulfilled. It also makes my mood a lot better. In January of 2020, I started school at Loyola. I started swimming again. In March of 2020, I was sent back to Michigan from New Orleans, my new city which was starting to feel like home and was becoming one of my favorite cities, and I was devastated. Because all in-person learning was paused due to the pandemic, there was no other option than to finish the semester in an online format. I do not understand the appeal of taking online classes, as I crave a real experience and people who I can talk to face-to-face. With the start of the pandemic, we were stuck inside and in isolation. I love alone time, but I also love spending time with my friends and people who live outside of where I am living. I am very social, and the beginning of the pandemic was so hard.

Worst of all, I had no place to swim, after recently realizing that swimming was such a key component of my life that I should never give up again. My mental health started to slip again. I started to spend lots of time sleeping. I wanted to feel numb. Now, the main thing I want is to feel.

Coming back from psychosis was one of the most difficult experiences of my life. I was still imagining sounds and putting meanings to those sounds that were untrue, and I found it very difficult to trust anyone. I remember one morning that I was sitting outside and the neighbors across the river were working on their house. I said, "Those are gunshots coming to kill me," to my mom. A different day, my mom took me for a drive on a dirt road because she knows that I love to do that, and I started freaking out and asking repeatedly if she was taking me to drop me off somewhere. Another day, I had a follow-up appointment at the hospital that my parents took me to, and I remember not believing them that I had an appointment. Instead, I once again thought they were taking me to drop me off and never pick me up again.

In addition to hallucinations and false beliefs, I was very overwhelmed by everything. As I mentioned in a different chapter, I was so overwhelmed by my phone. Most of my friends did not hear from me for about two weeks, and it took me about a month to start using my phone normally again. For weeks, the only people I saw were my close family members and my friends Carolyn, Morgan, and Logan. I was also overwhelmed by the coronavirus. At that point, wearing masks was new, and I was so nervous about all of it. I was afraid to leave the house, and that was a combination of the pandemic and of my idea that my parents would change the locks while I was gone. My story here is not in chronological order, as that time was very difficult to remember.

Since I had psychosis, my life has been different. I started to prioritize my mental health and the measures that make it better, and the main things are swimming and exercising in general. After it happened, I learned that there was the possibility of something like it happening to me again. I did not expect, however, to return to the hospital for mania less than six months later. After I had psychosis, I learned what therapy could do. I learned how much it could help me. I was paired with a therapist who explained everything to me in a scientific way or with lots of reason, and who was passionate about mindfulness and neuroscience.

There was also a stage of acceptance of all of it. I did not tell many people about what had happened, and in fact, I ended up mostly acting like nothing happened at all. It was not very hard to hide because the pandemic made life so different and more isolated anyways. I even had moments where I tried to convince myself that I had not had psychosis at all and that it must have just been a terrible panic attack. With my ill mind, I researched psychosis and found that many people experience visual hallucinations, which is something I barely experienced. I told myself that it just could not have been, ignoring that I had experienced every other symptom: auditory hallucinations, delusions, disorganized speech, and anxiety.

I eventually came to terms with the fact that I may have been having panic attacks during everything that happened, but that this escalated anxiety was a symptom of the bigger problem. With more acceptance came an increased sharing of my story. I never thought I would get psychosis, and I never thought that I would end up in the hospital for being so mentally unwell. If you are keeping any poison buried, stop trying to cover it up. Dig it up, let it out, and talk about it. My sunflowers could not grow and could not be healthy anymore with so much buried under them. There is no weakness in getting help with your mental health. People without mental illnesses can go to therapy too. It could change your life if you let it, no matter who you are.

The second time that I went to a psychiatric hospital was in September of 2020. I had a manic episode. The manic episode was a much more pleasant experience than the psychosis, although I am of the belief that the brief psychosis I was diagnosed with at the hospital in September was due to the ketamine I was injected with. I did not sleep for 96 hours before being taken to the hospital. On the day I was admitted to the hospital, every time I saw a mirror, I pointed in it, at myself, and started talking, yelling, or crying. I also had many moments during and leading up to the episode where I would cry with overwhelming happiness. I felt absolute euphoria. I felt so much, and it felt so good. I could not even tell that something was necessarily wrong because I felt so amazing. I went to the pool for a swim, and I had what felt like a revelation telling me I needed to write a book. I cried with happiness and took a picture of the pool to remember that exact moment. I met another swimmer there, and after I had told them my exciting news about writing a book, including in it the incredible impact that swimming has had on my life, I called my mom to tell her, too.

During my manic episode, I came up with the entire idea for this book. My mind was moving faster than it ever had before. I realized that so many of the things I am interested in and could even write a book about are all interconnected in a way, and they all make up the things that attract me. I thought about how I had lots of stories to share. I have my own stories, and I have the stories of others, and with all of these, I have compiled this memoir for you. I created this book because I wanted to, but also to give others the opportunity to hear these stories. I hope that people can relate to this book in some way, and if they do relate, I want them to know that they are not alone.

When I had the manic episode, the first people who came to my apartment were the police. There was no mental health professional around. I started yelling at the police because I was manic and getting very frustrated with them, and they ended up putting me in handcuffs and having me lay on the floor on my back. Soon after, the paramedics came and injected me with ketamine. I believe that I got my second psychosis from that ketamine because they did not know that I am very sensitive to some medications.

After the ketamine, I was taken to the hospital. I do not remember much, but I do recall waking up in a hospital bed in the emergency room. I was later sent to the psychiatric hospital, but I do not remember going there. I do not remember much from the first 24 hours, and my mom was not allowed to be contacted by the psychiatric hospital until I contacted her first. To add to it, they were not able to ask me or my mom questions since I was so out of it, so they were giving me a medication that made me feel like a zombie. When I finally started to wake up, it was around 10 am the next day. I told them I could no longer take the med they were giving me, and I called my mom. I started crying because I wanted some crayons or something to write with, and I ended up making a scene. Because of how I acted, I got injected with a shot to calm me down, something they sometimes must do in the psychiatric hospital. In the end, I got the crayons and notebook that I wanted.

Once I got the crayons and the journal, I started writing. I drew a lot, too. I have some of the drawings displayed in my room still. Many of the ideas I wrote in the journals are written about in this book. I filled up a notebook and a half in five days. The start of the notebook looks similar to the end of my notebook that contains the ideas and chapters for this book. It is chaotic and the writing is mainly in capital letters, with sentences that do not make any logical sense. The first journal from the hospital started to look more organized in the middle of it, but it is different than anything I would have made if I were not in the mental state or the place I was in. One of the pages has an ivy leaf that I asked a friend to color in. He colored each leaf with a different color. In my journal, I wrote about the things that made me feel euphoria. I wrote about the conversations I had with the other people there, and they wrote down their names so I could remember them.

I met many amazing people in the psychiatric hospital. I met people at their lowest of lows. I met another person who was at the end of a manic episode. I met a man who was schizophrenic. I met people who were days or hours out of a suicide attempt. A psychiatric hospital is a place where people are expected to heal in some way. We had each other as support. I got to know people who I never would have met and meeting them in the state they were in gave me a whole new understanding of life. I loved singing to uplift people's spirits and teaching my new friends why and how I did yoga in the mornings. I told them that I could see the light inside of them, because I could see it. It was shining bright.

I also met and talked a lot with the workers on the floor. The area where we ate was partly outside but had a ceiling and fence around the edges with long blue panels blocking people from seeing inside or out. That room was the only time we went out in the fresh air while we were at the hospital. I wanted to go outside so badly, and I wrote about it multiple times in my journal. When I finally left after a long five days, I danced and ran out of the hospital. I was so happy to be outside again. There was a worker in the dining room who found out that I loved to sing, and she brought in a battery-powered microphone the next day. She said, "Sing us a song." I sang "City of Stars" from the movie *La La Land*. She made my experience much better.

I also talked to one of the workers who seemed to supervise all parts of the floor. His name was like my brother's, and because of that I immediately had a connection with him. I talked with him whenever he was working, and he even started to feel like a friend. I would ask him questions about why things were the way that they were on the floor, and he would tell me the truth. One day, I saw him coloring something and told him that it was very pretty, and he showed me more. One of them was a beautiful and very colorful mandala. He had cut it out so that the paper was just the circle. I told him how much I loved it, so he gave it to me and signed his name on the back. I hung it up with a piece of tape on the window in my room at the hospital. I liked the way it looked when the sun shined through it in the mornings. I also hung up the mandala in my bedroom, and it is a reminder of a person who made my experience much happier.

One of the main goals at a psychiatric institute is to find the right medications so that people can function normally. For me, they tried a mood stabilizer. The morning I woke up after taking it for the first time, I felt like I was walking on a cloud. I briefly felt euphoria again. I could tell that the medication was going to work for me. When I was finally better, five days later, my parents came to pick me up. I was so excited; I had all my things including my new art and journals that I will never forget. With me, I also brought a few bracelets that I made in the art hour, the only time of the day where we got to make art and listen to music.

I think that the hardest part of coming back from it was coming to terms with the fact that something like that happened to me again, that I ended up in the psychiatric hospital for the second time. It is hard to come to terms with having to go there at all. I think, though, that I learned a lot about myself. I learned that I am worth the hard times because the people who love me still love me even though all this happened. From this, I have learned that if you radiate positivity, compassion, and love onto others, it will come back to you. I think my year of healing has also taught me that the things that have happened to me have made me a stronger, kinder, and wiser person.

I have learned not to blame myself for the mania and psychosis that I experienced. With anything that goes wrong with your mind, it is easy to judge yourself for it and wonder why your brain cannot just behave normally, but you can also just accept that sometimes the brain does odd things. Brains take strange turns sometimes. I realize that even though I went to a psychiatric hospital twice in 2020, I am still worth the same amount, and I am still worthy of the same love and happiness as before.

I have been able to grow from having a manic episode and from psychosis because they both brought me to writing. When I had psychosis, it was difficult to talk but I could journal. When I was manic, I wanted to write this book. I felt like writing was calling me. Writing is like therapy, and it allows me to dig deep within myself to find roots I did not even know existed. I have learned so much about myself by writing this book. I also grew from going to the mental hospital and meeting other people who were in similar situations as I was. I believe that I came out of 2020 kinder, more empathetic, and wiser. I grew because of what I experienced. We can grow anywhere, including in harsh conditions and against all odds. We can grow for the rest of our lives.

WHO SHOULD RESPOND?

TRIGGER WARNING: Sexual assault, mania, psychosis, police violence

Sometimes, we stretch ourselves too thin. We try to do too much at once. Some people take on too much work or too many jobs, and some people invest so much time into something that they no longer have much time to spend with the people in their lives. I believe that just as we stretch ourselves too thin, the police in the U.S. are also stretched too thin. They have too many jobs. They are expected to handle every single emergency, even if they might not be the best fit for the job. Police handle the roads and crimes, but they also are the first to respond to mental health crises.

Why were the police the first people who responded when I was having a manic episode? I had not slept in 96 hours. They were the first people to come to the scene to help me. I have a fear of the police. I do not fear the actual people who are police, but I fear the entire idea of police and how they act when they put their uniforms on. When they put on their uniforms, they often impose fear and escalate situations that are already escalated in the first place. Why do the police officers not bring guns on the mental health floor but bring them to the scene when they are called for a mental health emergency? Why did the police, not mental health professionals, respond when I was manic?

Why was it that when I repeatedly screamed, "Take me to my sunroom," where I knew there was a mattress where I could lay, the police did not do it? I knew I could feel so much calmer if I went there. I knew how great it would feel to lay down in a bed. Instead, the police put me in handcuffs and had me laying on the ground on my back. All I wanted was to be in the sunroom. Was that request really so hard? Why is it that when they have the option to use a taser, they use a gun? They seem to use the more intense options and techniques.

When the police came after my roommates called for help, and in my manic state, I wanted to teach the police a lesson. I felt intimidated the minute they walked into the apartment, but I also felt so powerful and knew that I was going to write this book. I knew that they saw me as simply a manic white 20-year-old girl. I tried to get them to use an alternative other than handcuffing me and injecting me with ketamine. I wanted the police to learn that I personally do not respond well to the things they were doing to me. I wish they also would have known that I had suffered psychosis before and that I am sensitive to some medications, before injecting me with a tranquilizer which I believe gave me psychosis for the second time. I was not afraid to be heard. Thinking back on it, if I were not a 20-year-old white female, things could have turned out much worse for me.

I wanted to be taken to the sunroom because I wanted to read and share with the police some of the journaling I had been doing as well as my mantras about treating people with respect and love, and about treating people like plants. As I said before, I knew I could teach them something. After not being granted this, and instead, being left on the ground in handcuffs laying on my back, I asked to be wrapped in a blanket tightly because I knew that would calm me down. They did not listen. I wish they would have listened. Could a mental health professional do a better job at calming people down than the police can?

At one point, I said, "Do you know what this feeling reminds me of?" They stared at me. They stared at me like I was an animal in a zoo. I said, "It reminds me of my sexual assault." They made me feel powerless and helpless, just like I had felt in 2018. After I said that, the majority of them still did not listen. There was one, however, who I believe had studied psychology. I know this because in my fearlessness I asked each one of the police officers who were in my apartment about their qualifications and what kind of education they had. I was genuinely curious, and I was manic, so I was freely saying whatever words came to mind. The one who I remember saying they studied psychology was listening to me. This police officer was flinching in response to my movements, and I could see them almost trying to stop what was happening and let me go into the sunroom. I love sunrooms, and I always have. I love to be in places where it is bright and sunny and where I feel alive. I did not feel alive handcuffed, laying on my back on the floor in a living room of an apartment.

I find it noteworthy that the police officer who studied psychology was more responsive, more attentive, and easier to talk to than the others. Based on my experience, I think that the police force as a whole could benefit greatly from having more training in psychology. I also think they should have to take implicit bias tests and implicit bias training. I think police officers should generally learn more about psychology and social justice so that they understand people better. Some of the degrees that I think would be helpful for police officers to have include social sciences, criminal justice, law, psychology, or public safety leadership. If police are going to have less than a years' worth of training, they should not be granted with the guns and weapons that they appear to have immediately. They should have to put in the time to have this kind of power.

I want it to be known that I do not hate the police. I have met nice, responsible, and respectful police officers. People pretend that mean people do not exist, with their only support to this statement being that they know so many nice people. Many do this with police officers. Just because you might know a nice officer does not mean that there are not police who are willing to murder people based on the color of their skin. Say their names. Rest in peace to those lives that were taken so unjustly. I feel most connected to the story of Elijah McClain because I was also injected with ketamine. What did not happen to me, however, was that Elijah was placed in a chokehold before being injected, and when he was injected, he was injected with far too much. In fact, Elijah was injected with so much ketamine that it killed him.

The police saw a black man that supposedly looked suspicious walking at night. What they did not know, however, was that Elijah was on his way home from a store. He was just dancing to his music, and he was cold because he was anemic. He was 23 years old when he died, and he was a massage therapist in Colorado who played violin for kittens. They did not know that the things Elijah wanted were to practice love, better himself every day, and change the world. In fact, Elijah influenced the world so much that he did change the world. I hate that this happened to Elijah, and I hate that people did not stand up for him. However, I do not hate all police.

I think that police need to be held to a higher standard. I do not think we should completely defund or abolish the police. We need some form of police, but perhaps the police do not need as much funding as they currently have. Perhaps they do not need as many responsibilities as they currently have. If some tasks were dedicated to mental health professionals, there would be fewer tasks assigned to the police and in turn, they might need less funding. This should be the idea behind defunding the police. It should not be about getting rid of the police, and it should not be about abolishing the police. It should be about the reallocation of funds and tasks. There were so many police officers at the scene when I had a manic episode and not a single mental health professional. This balance could be different. If the balance of officers and mental health professionals was different, some funding would be going to the mental health professionals instead of to the officers. If anything, we need more mental health professionals who can accompany the police. We need people speaking up for the people. We simply need a better system.

Police are given too many responsibilities. When I talked to people about the idea for this chapter and shared my experience with them, I told them how I believe a person trained in psychology or psychiatric emergencies should be sent to a mental health crisis. They agreed, then asked me something along the lines of, "How would we have the resources to do that?" The answer is that the allocation of resources and funds in this country is not anywhere close to being efficient. We need a reallocation of resources and money.

Imagine if mental health professionals were sent to mental health emergencies. In reality, it could help make the situation safer to have a police officer as backup, but the police officer should not be the first to respond. In my mind, I can imagine a mental health emergency because I have lived it. I dream that one day, mental health professionals will be the ones to respond first. Instead of escalating the situation and agitating the person having a crisis, like the police can do, mental health professionals could deescalate situations and help the person feel calmer. I picture the police being there for safety reasons, but maybe the police could stay in their car near the scene in case they are needed. Imagine if that police officer waiting nearby was required to have knowledge about psychology and training for mental health emergencies.

Why is it that police impose fear? Shouldn't we feel protected by the police? Why did I panic even more when the police arrived at my apartment during a manic episode instead of feeling like I was safe and going to be helped? One thing I know is that police often add a variable to an already tense situation, which can escalate it instead of diffusing or decreasing the tension. Police should be able to solve disputes and deescalate situations.

I do not hate all police. I do not believe in completely abolishing or defunding the police. I believe in something more lavender, which is reform. I believe in change. I think police are given too many responsibilities. Something is wrong when people are being killed by the police with this frequency. Something is wrong when the police are the first to respond to mental health emergencies. Something is wrong. Police officers have tasers and they have handcuffs that they can choose to use instead of guns. They also have their words. Those who should respond should treat people with kindness. Those who should respond should treat people like plants.

MEDITATIONS

Too often, people assume that meditation involves only sitting or lying down and being completely still and clear-minded. In practice, meditation is spiritual and it is more about awareness of the mind than the clearing of the mind. It is not necessarily stillness. Your mind may wander, and you must be okay with it. While meditating, you can let your thoughts come and go like the waves of an ocean. Meditations might be movement meditations, like walking, swimming, and yoga. When practiced regularly, meditations can change our lives for the better. Meditating can help us feel present and calm. These feelings can last much longer than the duration of the meditation.

We are capable of practicing awareness at more times than we realize. We can meditate by doing things that we enjoy. There are many different types of meditation. According to Mindworks, a meditation course, there are six different types of meditation: spiritual, mindfulness, movement, focused, visualization, and chanting. [18] Some sources say that there are fewer or more than six types of meditation, but I picked these six because they are the main forms I have practiced. One of the most effective meditation types for me is movement meditation. No form of meditation is necessarily better than another, but one form might work better for you than another. Meditation takes practice and the dedication of time to better oneself. Meditation can lead to self-awareness and harmony with oneself, which could lead to a happier life.

Spiritual meditation is a meditation form where the person who is doing it is trying to connect with something higher than oneself. Something higher than oneself could be a higher power, the universe, the Earth, or one's higher self. When I meditate, I try to connect with the Earth. One of the ways I do that is by sitting on the ground. Sitting on the ground makes me feel much more grounded and closer to the Earth, which is something that I consider to be a higher power. Spiritual meditation can contain a prayer, silent or spoken, but it does not need to. People practice spiritual meditations in places of worship and in nature, but they also can be practiced anywhere.

Mindfulness meditation is the form that comes to mind when many people think of meditation, and it originates from Buddhism. In this form of meditation, one must work with concentration and awareness. Contrary to what people may believe, you do not need to clear your mind in mindfulness meditation. It is actually the opposite of that. Mindfulness is about awareness, and in this form of meditation you should not judge the thoughts that come into your mind, but instead let them come and go with ease. If you have anxiety, I highly suggest mindfulness meditation. When you are young, it can help strengthen your frontal cortex, which is the part of your brain that should help you come up with a rational response to situations. If you struggle with anxiety or panic attacks, strengthening the frontal cortex can help.

My favorite way to practice mindfulness meditation is to sit in a comfortable position, which for me is often sitting cross-legged on the ground because it makes me feel close to the Earth. In mindfulness meditation, a person first acknowledges what is around them and they check in with all their senses. In mindfulness, you think about all five of your senses. The next thing to do in mindfulness meditation after observing everything around you is to observe everything inside of you. You can check in on how you are feeling. You can check in on your thoughts and let them come and go without judgement. Something that people talk about in yoga is an ocean-like breath. Something else that is ocean-like is your thoughts. They are like the waves of an ocean because you can let them come and go without judgement. You do not judge what comes in or what comes out, you just let your thoughts move. The next thing to do in mindfulness meditation is to bring yourself back once you start to wander or drift off. You can bring yourself back to your breath or the senses you are experiencing. You can find a sense of ease in your mind, body, and soul. Mindfulness meditation is about awareness, your breath, and everything going on around and inside of you.

After my psychosis episode, I worked with a life-changing therapist who taught me about meditating. I still use the techniques he gave me. He taught me about mindfulness meditation. When I had psychosis, I would do therapy sessions in the area next to my bedroom and underneath the deck at my parent's house. The room is right by the river and the birds chirp loudly. My therapist would tell me to first focus on my breathing, then on everything around me, then again on my surroundings. I would listen to the birds, look at the trees, take in the sun, and smell the fresh Michigan summer air. Under that deck was where much of my healing took place. Another place I healed was in the forest. The beauty of the trees and gentle sun peeking through always gives me a sense of calm as I walk the forest trails.

A different way I learned how to meditate from my therapist that summer was to hold ice cubes in both of my hands and breathe deeply. This works very well for me during panic attacks. The cold feeling can calm the nervous system and make one feel a lot less anxious. I highly recommend trying this when you are feeling very uneasy or panicked. People who struggle with anxiety might also struggle with insomnia. A technique that I love to use for insomnia is progressive muscle relaxation. Progressive muscle relaxation is where you relax your body little by little from the bottom to the top or from the top to the bottom.

One of the main benefits of mindfulness meditation, as I mentioned earlier, is that it can help with anxiety. Mindfulness meditation can also improve a person's attention abilities. Research has shown that more meditation is linked to less habituation, which is the decrease in the response to a stimulus after the stimulus has been repeatedly presented. Additionally, meditation can improve attention abilities because it can help decrease the wandering of the mind. [19]

I do not think enough people realize that movement meditation is a form of meditation. Movement meditation includes swimming, a walk in the woods, gardening, stretching, yoga, and many other activities. Movement meditation is all about focusing on what is happening with the mind and the body, while still moving the body. My favorite movement meditation is swimming. My second favorite is cooking. My dad taught me my way around the kitchen, which became one of my favorite places to meditate. For as long as I can remember, my dad and I baked together. Every year, we make piles and piles of Christmas cookies together. I feel a sense of belonging when I am in the kitchen. I feel the ability to be creative while following a routine. I can use as much or as little spice as I would like to, and I can add additional ingredients that I think will fit. My favorite ingredient is cilantro. Cilantro is part of two types of foods I love the best, which are Mexican food and Thai food. The flavor is so prominent and delicious, and without it, many foods could never live up to their full potential in my eyes.

I also feel a sense of belonging when I am in the pool. Swimming is the best meditation that I have ever found for myself. There is a magic to the sound and the feeling of the water when I move through it. One of my favorite places to go swimming in is a small, peaceful lake near my parent's house. There is a beautiful trail that one must first hike to reach this clear, quiet lake. The circumference of the lake is about a mile, so I swim the perimeter of it. Something else I love just as much as swimming and cooking is walking. I like being on a trail among the trees or where I can see mountains. I like to be in places that make me feel big and small at the same time.

I also love to do yoga as a movement meditation. I started doing yoga in high school and quickly learned that it is one of my favorite movement meditations other than swimming. It reminds me of swimming because a person must move their entire body to perform the act. I love swimming and yoga. I love how they feel. I think it is incredible that I am able to do something like that with my body and it allows me to practice a lot of gratitude for that. In yoga and swimming, you use many limbs to make the movements. One of my favorite things about yoga is using muscles that I do not normally use. In yoga, a person stretches parts of the body that do not normally get stretched. In doing this, I create space.

I create space in my mind and my body. I believe that creating space occurs in many types of movement meditations. People will tell you that yoga is best if it is practiced often and will talk about doing yoga every day. I think that people who can do movement meditations should do them every day. If we have the capability to, we should move every day. I love movement meditations and trying to understand my body during them.

In the previous chapter, I wrote about how police officers are expected to do too much. I think that people expect themselves to do too much. There are some things that we can do to slow down and stop trying to multi-task all the time. One of those things we can do is focused meditation. Focused meditation is about bringing your mindfulness to something simple. My favorite thing to do during focused meditation is to have a cup of coffee. When I take that first sip, I think about the way the warmth makes my body feel and I think about the taste. I think about the different flavors and components in the coffee. I think about how the beans came from the Earth. When I am doing a focused meditation while drinking a cup of coffee, I can think about only the coffee. Focused meditation is about bringing your attention to one specific thing. When your mind wanders, you bring it back to the simple thing that is going on. Similar to other meditations, when your mind starts to wander, you bring it back to something else.

Visualization meditation was the first meditation I was introduced to, and it has been one of the most beneficial meditations I have learned. It has specifically helped me in swimming. For someone who wants to try this meditation in a simple form, I recommend trying to visualize a place that makes you feel very happy and peaceful. Places I would imagine are being in a forest, a beach, or a mountain. Visualizing these things will bring you to that place in a way. Daydreaming, as I have written before, is a type of traveling. It allows you to see something in your mind.

Visualization meditation can be used when you have a goal. This is connected to spiritual meditation because it is imagining yourself at the point where you have achieved your goals. This is a higher version of yourself because it is where you want to see yourself. I first did visualizations when I was 10 years old. The way I have done this is by starting with progressive muscle relaxation. I do this relaxation with my eyes closed while laying down and focusing on my breathing. I visualize myself on the pool deck, putting on my cap and goggles, and stepping up on the starting block. I visualize the race from start to finish doing the best I ever have. When I was 12 years old, I visualized myself swimming a 200 breaststroke with a specific time goal many times. When I finally swam that race at the state meet that I wanted to win, I went the exact time that I visualized so many times. I believe that visualization meditation has worked wonders for me since I started doing it.

Chanting meditation is about mantras as well as mindfulness. This form of meditation is like a previous one I described, mindfulness meditation. The difference between the two is that when your mind starts to drift into thought in chanting meditation, you bring it back to a mantra. The way to practice chanting meditation is to meditate with the repetition of a word, phrase, or sound. These can be mantras, intentions, goals, or anything that can be repeated and meditated with. The first time I tried chanting meditation was at a yoga class while repeating "om". Everyone sat with their eyes closed and their hands at their heart's center. We all repeated "om" in unison three times. It made me feel a sense of community to do this in unison with everyone and it also felt very calming to say "om" three times, holding it out each time. I think that chanting meditations can be very beneficial when something meaningful is repeated.

It is necessary to keep in mind that meditation cannot fix everything that has to do with mental health issues. In fact, meditation has not been shown to improve depression for everyone who has it, even if they are trained on how to meditate properly. Often, depression will not be improved without the help of professionals. Meditation should be something additional that one does to take extra care of themselves and their mind.

Near my parent's home, there is a lovely forest with a hiking trail. I learned the power of meditating in a forest there. I also learned about it at my favorite parks in Ann Arbor and New Orleans. I learned about quietly sitting at a bench and following the meditation that I had learned in the summer of 2020. I have found that it is best to do it outside. I have guided a few friends through these meditations, and I have seen how much calmer they are when it is finished. I believe that the forest is a healer. I love going to parks. I like walking, sitting, picnicking, and meditating in parks. I like meditating in them because I can listen to the birds, water, rustling of the trees, and everything around me. Parks make me feel close to the plants and the Earth, and they make me feel alive.

After listing all of these different types of meditations, I want to stress that movement meditation might be the most enjoyable way for you to see the benefits of regular meditation. In movement meditation, you can do something you enjoy, such as walking, gardening, or even cooking, and you can fully immerse yourself in what you are doing. You can be mindful of everything that is going on in and around you. Try to give yourself time every single day. A great way to do this is through movement meditation.

A wonderful activity that brings similar advantages as meditation is journaling. Journaling can bring a person into the present moment and can make them more mindful. It can also simply be a great way to write down your ideas as they come to you instead of just trying to remember them. Writing inspires creativity. For as long as I can remember, I have had journals to write in, and sometimes I have multiple journals that I write in during the same period. One of my favorite journals to keep is a list journal, which contains my day-to-day to-do lists as well as some creative and fun lists.

I believe that people who have addictive personalities can use meditation to their advantage. People with addiction issues form habits easily, but they may also find that they can form healthy habits easily, too. Examples of healthy habits are working out, journaling, practicing gratitude, walking, and having a good sleep schedule. People with addictive personalities may find that they can form the habit to do these things regularly and that it is not so hard to form the habit. A great habit to form is meditation, and as I wrote about in this chapter, meditation does not have to be just one thing. Meditation comes in many different forms.

To me, meditation is about releasing. There are so many beautiful ways to meditate, and it can help with anxiety. It can also help with insomnia and generally being calmer. I believe in the power and the beauty of meditating. I think it can truly change a person's life. I know how I feel when I swim, walk in a forest, and cook. I feel mindful and mindless, at the same time. I feel bliss.

THE LEADERS OF THIS COUNTRY AND THE WORLD

The leaders of this country during this pandemic era are healthcare workers. These are the people who give care even when it means they might die because they are going to work. Healthcare workers risk their lives for the common good of humanity and because they are needed on the battlefield of public health. Some of the most important healthcare workers in my life have been mental health professionals. Additional examples of leaders are changemakers, intellectuals, scientists, great police, and governmental leaders.

On the day before 9-11-2020, which was also the day before I was released from the hospital after a long five days there, which was a shorter stay than many other patients, I sang "The Star-Spangled Banner". I stood in my doorway and pointed to the nurses and sang about them. I sang about healthcare workers. I sang about the ones who fought the coronavirus before we even knew that most patients do not need ventilators, before we knew how effective masks were, and when hospitals feared not having enough room to care for all the patients who were infected and at a high risk of death. I sang about these bright stars who fought through perilous times. I sang about the ones who showed that our country still is the home of the brave because they are the brave. They are the stars of the pandemic. I have always had a lot of respect for healthcare workers, but this respect intensified immensely when seeing and hearing about what they were going through and doing throughout 2020. It also intensified when I needed mental health help more than I ever knew I could need it. Nurses, doctors, respiratory therapists, mental health professionals, and all other hospital and medical workers often have a huge selfless desire to help others. The ones who truly care about people and humanity as a whole are the ones who excel.

I felt so much pride singing that song for the first time in four years. "The Star-Spangled Banner" was written after a U.S. fort was bombed by British ships during the War of 1812. "The Star-Spangled Banner" was a celebration of U.S. victory. It did not become the national anthem until over 100 years later in 1931. I have always loved singing acapella, and I sang "The Star-Spangled Banner" at swim meets for the whole deck and audience to hear for as long as I can remember. People knew I sang it at swim meets, and sometimes I would go to other pools for away meets and someone would find me on deck and ask if I would sing it. I felt so much pride when singing the song at the hospital. I felt pride because I was singing to nurses. I told them that they had bright lights inside them.

My stay at the psychiatric hospital changed my life. I learned so much about psychology and the power of positive reinforcements. I also met people who were days, or even hours, out of trying to take their own lives. I learned about myself. I took a break from my phone. I sang, I drew, and I wrote. I learned from the people I met.

I met amazing healthcare workers who changed my life when I was in the psychiatric hospital for the second time. I asked them about their experience on the unit during the beginning of the COVID-19 pandemic, and they told me about how scared they were but that on the unit, only patients who were negative for the virus could come. On that unit, the patients were not expected to wear masks because of this. Only the workers were required to wear masks, and they were tested for the virus often. They put their lives at risk by going to work while many people got to stay home when everything was so unknown around them. Meanwhile, healthcare workers walked into a hospital where a virus was taking over essential care areas of the hospital, and where there were often not enough beds for the number of patients in the hospital. They knew that they could be called to work with the COVID patients due to a lack of staffing at any moment and that if it happened, they would be scared for their own health and life.

Mental health professionals are leaders of this country and the world. Great ones show how much they care about the well-being of people. Therapists and psychiatrists can save lives. I know I could have gotten stuck having psychosis and mania for longer than I did if I did not have the access to the medications and help that I had. I have a lot of respect and I feel very thankful for mental health professionals. I think we must normalize getting their help even more in this world. We can normalize that needing help is part of life.

Intellectuals are also the leaders of this country and this world. Many intellectuals are scientists. It has been scientists and healthcare workers who have been working to bring this world back to a more normal state, slowly but surely. We can now see that changes do not happen overnight with this kind of a thing. Our patience has been tested, but there are people we can trust, and there are facts that we can trust. This security comes from the ideas, practices, and discoveries of intellectuals.

Great leadership is essential, and it is not the easiest thing to find. Political leaders must be great for a country to come back from a pandemic, and business leaders must be great to lead their business and their people through a pandemic. There have been so many examples of leaders cutting the wages of everyone except their own, or only cutting their wages slightly but cutting the rest drastically. Great business leaders know that people need to be paid fairly and that they should have done everything in their power to keep paying their employees as expected when the pandemic began. Great business leaders also know that their employees needed extra understanding and empathy as it is not easy to switch to a lifestyle of working from home and being isolated.

Great police are leaders of this country. I have a lot of respect for police who studied psychology and social justice. My friend Jasper, who saw me during the end of my manic episode, told me that great police are positive, vibrant, and social people. They know when there is a threat and when there is not a threat. I believe that great police understand people and how to talk to people. Jasper agrees that we should not defund the police, but instead there should be a reallocation of resources. We need change. We need lavender.

There is an idea that my friend Jasper taught me about. It is the idea of star children. Star children are simply as they sound: people who come from the stars. When someone is referred to as a star in athletics or entertainment, it usually means they are the best of the best. Star children are similar, but they are the stars of the universe. They are sent from the stars on a mission to better the world for all. They are made to make the world a better place with their existence. Jasper called me a star child, and after he explained the meaning to me, I do not think there are much higher compliments. I believe that great leaders are star children.

I have a very good friend who I believe could change the world in a very good way. Ryan, my friend from Lindenwood University, told me that his goal is to work for the Fed (the Federal Reserve). He wants to work for the Fed because he feels like it is something that people often overlook, and it makes such an impact on the lives of Americans. The Fed has the power and the ability to push money in the directions of impoverished communities and provide help to people. He wants to feel like he is part of the center of all the finances in America. He wants to create an impact on small levels that create rippling effects.

Great leaders will change the world. Like many people, I like to surround myself with people who make this world a better place. I often feel like these people are leaders. They are not afraid to speak up for what they believe in. They are not afraid to be heard, and they are not afraid to share their ideas. I also like to surround myself with star children. I believe that those who live by the mantra of making this world a better place with their existence are the ones who will make a difference.

LEADING WITH A FEMININE APPROACH

Men can be feminine, just as women can be masculine. Men can be more in tune with their feminine characteristics, and I think it can also help them with leadership. This chapter is about how both men and women can lead with a feminine approach. Leading with a feminine approach encompasses being compassionate and understanding while focusing on uplifting others. As more women step into top leadership roles, such as the role of being president of this country, men will learn more and more about how to lead like a woman.

An article from Harvard Business Review explains leadership lessons that men can learn from women. As Chamorro-Premuzic and Gallop explain, there are too many unethical, narcissistic, and overconfident people in leadership roles. [20] Because most leadership roles are currently taken by men, some may think that this suggests that men are better leaders and that because of it, they take the majority of the leadership roles. The truth is that women were held back for far longer than men. They are still held back. The year 2020 marked 100 years of women having the right to vote. A woman did not become a presidential candidate until 1872 when Victoria Woodhull became the first female candidate nearly 100 years after the U.S. had its first president. When she ran for president, women were not even able to vote her in.

The article argues that women understand flaws, weaknesses, and limitations better than men. This is linked to the studies that have shown that women show less overconfidence than men. Chamorro-Premuzic and Gallop argue that because of this self-awareness, women can prepare better as well as understand when they want to improve in an area where they are lacking. [20] Women also tend to put others ahead of themselves. Likewise, women do not tend to be as self-focused as men. Great leaders do not lead with selfishness, and they are not narcissistic. Some people only want to be leaders to benefit themselves and are often only striving for the money. Great leaders bring people together, put them first, and uplift them. Women are very capable of doing this, and they may find this instinctive trait in their ability to raise a family.

Women often lead with more kindness and empathy than men do. They also often lead with a transformational approach, which means that they strive to inspire and appeal to people's hearts and souls. Transformational leadership is linked to productivity and engagement. Women lead in this way because of their emotional intelligence. There is a reason that so many women work in people-oriented jobs like teaching and nursing. Because women lead with empathy, they understand that people are humans, not robots. I have seen this in swimming with coaches, as I have noticed that in my experience, female coaches tend to be easier to talk to and more understanding. I have seen male coaches who seemed to think that people can behave like robots. I have also seen male coaches who are very understanding, and I have swam under a male coach who gives his athletes mental health days when they need them.

Something I want to get across in all of these chapters about femininity and female power is that men have feminine characteristics. An issue we often see is that men are afraid to let their feminine characteristics shine. The truth of the matter is that men can learn from women. Men can learn from the way that women lead, which involves the way they naturally treat others.

Because of what I have learned from my own life experiences and from Concepción Arenal, I think that women make incredible leaders. I also think that men who are great leaders often have feminine qualities. The greatest feminine leaders lead with compassion, empathy, humility, and resilience. A study by Pew Research Center found that half of the respondents say women are more honest than men, 80% say that women are more compassionate than men, and 60% say that women are more creative than men. [21] All three of these characteristics make great leaders and especially great political leaders. I think that the future is feminine.

Just as there are great feminine political leaders, there are also great feminine family leaders. A family leader is not necessarily the member of the family who makes the most money. In a two-parent home, there is often a parent who works more or makes more than the other one, and thus becomes the breadwinner of the family. The breadwinner, however, is not always the most influential. Oftentimes, one parent is not able to work outside of the home because they are busy raising children. The parent who spends more time with the children often understands them better and has more time to give them the affection, love, and time that they need to grow. It is often seen that the breadwinner is the leader of the family, but the true leader of the family may the one who offers the most love and care. None of this means that the breadwinner must be male, and that the primary caregiver must be female. It can be any way.

The managers of the hotel where I worked for a summer internship were powerful women. They were women who had trust from others, and everyone in the hotel recognized that the managers knew how to handle every situation. They worked together to solve problems. Additionally, the HR managers were both women. HR managers are more often women. There are reasons that this occupation is dominated by women. HR managers make sure everyone feels safe to talk about any issues regarding the managers and other employees, and they also must not be afraid to speak up when something is not right.

The managers of the ice cream shop I worked in every summer at the end of high school and beginning of college were also powerful women. They taught me so much about leadership and especially about leading with positivity. My first manager at the ice cream shop was also the captain of my high school swim team, and it was she who felt I was capable of shift leading before I even started working there. I remember feeling so overwhelmed when she led me through managing the closing of the shop, but I soon had the feeling I knew how to close that ice cream shop as well as I knew how to swim.

My first manager taught me the ropes of how to lead the ice cream shop, but also how to be a leader who made people feel good about themselves.

After the first summer of working at the ice cream shop, I had a new manager. Her name is Alivia. Alivia taught me about myself. We both started working there in the summer of 2017, and we immediately had a great relationship as co-workers. When Alivia became the manager, she still saw me as her co-worker, or her equal. We learned about leadership together, as a team. She learned about her employees, and one of those employees was me, while her employees learned about and from her. One of Alivia's mantras as a leader is, "We are equals, we are in it together, we are a team." She told me that she never saw herself as someone who was above me but instead felt that she was in a place where she had the ability to empower others. She thinks that in a team, everyone can learn to trust each other, and they can learn that everyone has something different to offer.

She wanted her employees to learn that it was never all about ice cream, but instead about building relationships and learning about yourself. She wanted to build relationships with all of her employees so they could have mutual respect and so they could possibly have someone to look up to. It is easier to talk to a friend than to a manager. She told me how honored she was that I thought of her to write about. I was impacted greatly by Alivia and genuinely thought about what she said when I interviewed her for this book, which was that if she positively impacted even one person with her leadership so far, it was all worth it. She impacted me positively with her leadership.

I have often thought about that in translation to writing this book. Even if it impacts just one person, writing over 50,000 words was all worth it.

Alivia believes that women should be in more leadership roles because we have been silenced for too long. It is not about being able to talk nor an issue with being empowered, but instead, it is about the fact that we simply should be in more leadership roles. It has nothing to do with men not being able to do a good job. Just because a woman is capable does not mean a man is not. She said to me, "If you understand a woman and her life, you will understand that she is fully capable. She juggles a lot, her life is different from a man's, but she is fully capable. She is a leader in her life every single day, and she could make a great leader of others."

Something that many women may hear is that they are too emotional. Being overly emotional is generally accepted as a negative feminine trait, but it does not have to be seen as such. It is not a bad thing to be emotional. I talked to Alivia about this topic, and she said that emotions are not negative traits, just like feminism is not a dirty word. Her definition of feminism is a little different than how I see it. She told me she thinks that feminism is not as simple as equality because women have always been human, which means they have been equal all along even if they have not been treated as such. Equal does not mean that there are not differences. In fact, there are many differences between men and women, and one of those differences is the willingness and capability of being emotional. It is unhealthy to shut out feelings, and it can cause us to be in conflict with ourselves if we do not let out our feelings somehow. I think that because Alivia is emotional, she is able to be more empathetic as a leader. Alivia considers every perspective. She is more able to navigate the feelings and emotions of others because she is emotional herself.

She told me that she sometimes gets called intimidating, aggressive, assertive, and dominant. She used to be ashamed of these characteristics that are often associated with masculinity until she learned that they are part of her just like her femininity is part of her, too. She spoke a lot about her inner goddess and divine femininity, and we talked about how some women are capable of having a child. There is something very divine about that. It took a lot of work for Alivia to become who she is today, and she has learned to take pride in all of her traits, feminine or otherwise.

I talked with my best friend, Carolyn, about feminism. She defines feminism as empowering, supporting, and believing in women. She says it is about being an advocate for women's rights. She graduated with a degree in engineering, so she is a woman in a male-dominated field. It is important to her that she makes the same amount of money as a man doing the same work. It is also important for her to see female leaders in her field. I asked Carolyn about leadership, and she told me that leaders are good listeners. She thinks great leaders listen to superiors and those under them. They are people who have empathy so they can relate to people.

She says great leaders are motivational. They must be able to support and keep people going. They must be rational and have logical thinking. It is easier to follow a leader who explains why they do what they do. They need to explain how they problem solve and what steps they take to get to where they are. We spoke about how for many people, the greatest leader they have in their life is their mother. Many people learn about leadership from their moms and the way she treats her family. Carolyn told me that her mother, who has become somewhat like another mother to me through all these years, was a good role model and leader for her from the start. Carolyn took on some of her mom's leadership traits. Carolyn explained that her mom is smart, compassionate, empathetic, and a good listener. She also told me that her dad is a great leader, too. Carolyn has always looked up to her parents.

Another place where I have learned about feminine leadership is through swimming. Swimming has taught me so much about friendship, and I have learned lessons about leadership from the great captains I have had. During my last year of swimming for Lindenwood University, my captain, Erin, was also one of my very good friends. Erin led by example. She wanted people to see her as a role model, and she wanted to primarily show her good attitude and good work ethic. I talked with Erin while I was writing this book, and she told me that she was inspired herself by inspiring others.

One of Erin's mantras is to have compassion. She believes in doing things that she is passionate about, and she believes in putting importance on the little things and the things that she does every day. Erin recently became a nurse, and she told me that she wanted to become a nurse because she has always believed in helping others. Additionally, she always found interest in the human body. She grew up Catholic and was taught about helping others and doing charity work. She now works with a Catholic organization that combines nursing with charity work and spiritual care. Erin told me that spiritual care is just as important as medicine. Someone Erin knows did a study on spiritual care and the findings of the study were that the group of cancer patients had a better outcome from chemotherapy if they had some kind of faith or practiced spiritual care. Spiritual care can be meditation, and people do not have to be religious to find spiritual care helpful. I believe that religions and spirituality can teach us that if we give something time and energy it will give back to us. Being spiritual helps us.

Erin believes that more women should be in leadership roles because they are underrepresented. It is important to advocate for equality where everyone has rights and opportunities that are equal to those of white males. Every group out there wants representation in leadership roles, but we should not simply put someone in a place of power only because they are a minority. We should put those people in the role because they are the best fit for the job. A woman should not become the CEO of a company just to show that a woman can do it, but instead because a woman can truly do it.

Referred to as the gender optimism gap, a poll from Healthways Research Center reported that 30% more women are optimistic about their futures than men are. [22] The estimated reason for this difference is that women are more likely to surround themselves with close friends, and that there is a positive correlation between more social interactions and being optimistic for women. It was also found that the ideal close circle of friends ranges from four to twelve people. It can be nice to have a small circle and more time to spread love and positivity to every friend you have. Being positive and optimistic can strengthen leadership. A leader must always have hope to be able to lead others.

In a previous chapter, I wrote about how women are more socially oriented than men, and I believe this helps them to be great leaders. Socially oriented people may find it easier than individually oriented people to have good relationships with others. Great leaders have good relationships with the people they are leading. In the dictator experiments reported on by Catherine C. Eckel and Philip J. Grossman, some dictators were given money to divide between themselves and an anonymous respondent. The idea of the experiment was that the more the dictator donated, the less selfish the respondent was. Women, on average, donated about twice as much as men did. Eckel and Grossman point out that women are different than men in mental disposition and they mention the tenderness and selflessness of women. The general conclusion of the experiment is that women are more socially oriented, and men are more individually oriented. [23]

I believe that because women are shown to be more socially oriented than men, they can use this attribute to be great leaders. I think we see this in the experiment as well as in politics. The majority of Democrats are women. Democrats tend to be more socialist and collectivistic than Republicans. An idea of the Republican party is to be more individualistic, leading men to be drawn to this political party. Capitalism is individualistic. Men are thought to emphasize power, competition, and dominance, all of which are individualistic things, whereas women are not. Women are thought to emphasize care and being accommodating and nurturing, all of which are traits more associated with being more collectivistic. In the 2020 election, Joe Biden had women to thank for his win, as 57% of women voted for him and only 45% of men did. [24]

I wrote about how people do not have to be all masculine or all feminine, and they do not have to possess characteristics associated with masculinity if they are male. Men can have many feminine traits, and I think that men can be better leaders if they embrace their femininity. I talked with a friend who I immediately thought about when I wrote this chapter, Gerald. Gerald and I were on the same team at Lindenwood University. When given some words to pick from, Gerald considers himself to be group-oriented, nurturing, and caring, all of which are associated with femininity. I asked Gerald if he is afraid of showing his feminine traits or being called feminine, and he told me that he was not because he sees all people as individuals, not male or female. He looks at people this way in sports and life.

We talked about how many coaches tend to coach men and women differently, but Gerald thinks they should all be coached as individuals. He thinks that coaches might think that being an athlete for the social aspect is more feminine and that being one for the competition and the drive is more masculine, but they should not treat this as black and white. Different people are athletes for different reasons, and it does not depend on their gender. We have not reached equality in sports. I have seen male coaches get blinded by outcome goals when the ultimate goal should be to increase confidence and build the best people that they can. Gerald told me that coaching swimming is about a lot more than just swimming. He coaches little kids and wants them to learn about who they are and build confidence much more than he wants them to swim fast.

Gerald sees everyone as an individual. He knows we are all different and that it is okay. As I say, we are different, but we are equal. Gerald told me that anyone can be a leader, no matter their gender, if they have the right traits to be a leader. When he is put in a leadership role, he strives to teach others that they get what they work for, that they should be proud of what they are doing, and to be confident. Gerald values input as a leader and he loves to get people to strive for one common goal. He believes that leaders should be cooperative and not controlling. Gerald's mantra came from his swim coach, and it is, "Practice makes performance." This means that who you are daily is who you will be in a stressful situation. You grow to be the person you are every day, and you must grow to be capable of handling tough situations.

I thought of Gerald when I wrote about leading with a feminine approach because he is someone I know who truly is a great leader who lets his feminine traits show and shine. I think it takes some of the characteristics he has to be a great leader, including being group-oriented, caring, and nurturing. I believe there are lessons that men can learn from women about leadership. Women can be capable of creating life, which makes me believe they must have some natural nurturing and leadership qualities.

Some things are special about women. As I described in the chapter about women having power, women can be capable of having children. They also live longer. I believe that women are more resilient than men. Because of this, I think that men and women can both learn from women in general. I think everyone can learn to lead with a feminine approach.

HOW BUSINESSES CAN TREAT PEOPLE LIKE PLANTS

I want to own my own business. Of all the aspects of business, I am most interested in HR (human resources) and finance. There is a very interesting connection between the CFO of a company and the human resources manager. I believe that the main intentions of a business should be to make people happy and to make money. It is very possible to make customers happy but to fail to bring happiness to the employees of a business. A company is not truly a good one if it does not treat its people correctly.

People have many needs. Their workplace should cater to these needs. Not only should it cater to needs, but it should also cater to wants. A business does not have much if its employees are not happy to work there. The best way to make employees happy is to have enough money to do so. In a business, money buys happiness. A successful business cannot have lousy finance and accounting departments. Great businesses make their money work for them. Great businesses also treat people like plants.

Every business has goals. One main goal for any business is to profit, and a business must be profitable to stay afloat. Next, a business should strive to create and keep customers. It should also try to attract and retain employees.

I believe that the best way to attract and keep people around in a business is to treat them fairly and to apply the principles of treating people like plants. Employees and customers can be treated like plants, just as your friends and loved ones can. In the Plants chapter, I wrote about how you can treat people like plants in general, and in this chapter, I have written specifically about how to treat employees and customers like plants.

Another goal of a business is to be innovative and to maximize resources. Efficient companies will be able to maximize their resources and in turn, will save time and money. If a business is efficient, it will not be investing time or resources into endeavors that are not getting to the end goal. Being inefficient holds businesses back from the things that really matter. Finally, one goal of every business is to grow in some way. A business can grow by hiring more employees, gaining customers, making new products, making new models of already existing products, and cutting costs.

There are goals that every business has, such as profit and gaining customers, and there are also goals that businesses should have but do not always have. These goals include benefiting society, practicing CSR (Corporate Social Responsibility), encouraging health, and making people happy. When businesses have these goals, they tend to be the types of businesses that treat people like plants. They understand that their businesses are about much more than profitability. A business that treats people like plants is a business that cares about the wellbeing of people and understands that it must provide its employees with fair wages, good working conditions, and good living conditions.

A business can benefit society by creating jobs. The business can benefit society even more if it provides fair wages for its employees. A business should always at least provide a livable wage that allows its employees to have safe housing and to afford food. Employees must be able to afford the cost of living that pertains to the area where the business is located. Another way that a business can benefit society is by providing a product or a service that people need. This benefits society even more if the product or service they provide is a reasonable price and is of good quality.

Businesses can treat people like plants. They can treat their employees and their customers like plants by listening and paying attention to them and their needs and then adapting for them. Sometimes, plants get overwatered. Some plants only need to be watered once a month, and if they are watered every day, they will die. It is easy to have the misconception that when a plant is dying it needs more water. As discussed in the Plants chapter, it might be the opposite. The plant might need less. This can be compared to contacting your customers too much. Let the customer decide what they want with your assistance, but do not push them too much. Just like pushing your customers too much, pushing your employees too much is unproductive. Overworking or micromanaging your employees is like giving them too much water or sunlight. It might feel like what you are doing is helping, but it likely is not. Let them grow how they need to grow.

I interviewed a good friend that I met at my first university, and we talked about the topics discussed in this chapter. Kenzie got her degree in human resources, so I knew that she would be a good person to talk to about businesses treating people like plants. Kenzie said that businesses can treat people like plants by creating a culture where people genuinely like going to work. They can treat people like plants by checking in on people. Kenzie emphasized how you never know what is going on in everyone's life. Something catastrophic could be going on in an employee's personal life but they still must go to work. Kenzie believes that great business leaders should check in on how their subordinates are doing. They should know if their employees are unwell and if there is anything they can do to help them. Leaders should not know all the details of a person's life at home, but they should understand that everyone has a life outside of work that they do not see. It is important to be mindful and aware of people and how they are doing.

Kenzie is a brand operations manager. She oversees the product life cycle, works on shipments, replenishes products, and makes sure other managers have all the staff and things they need to do their jobs. From her job, she has learned that everyone needs something different. Businesses must find a balance of catering to the needs of people while still being productive. Kenzie said, "You cannot always make people feel good, but you can make people feel better." Kenzie cares about people and makes them feel cared about, something that is a great quality to have as a leader.

She believes that companies can keep their employees happy by paying them enough. The pay must also be competitive. In a country that is based on economics, such as the U.S., it is nearly impossible for people to put how much they are being paid for doing their job in the back of their minds. Getting paid enough is crucial. Another way that Kenzie believes employees can be kept happy is if their expectations are laid out to them. Everyone must know the expectations of anything that is asked. Setting expectations early sets people up for success. If they do not know their expectations, you are setting them up for failure because communication is lost. Communication in business is essential.

I asked Kenzie about her mantras, and she told me that she lives by the idea of empowering herself and others. She works for a lingerie company and believes in the empowerment of all women. She also believes in empowerment as a leader. She thinks that it is important to empower your subordinates. This will help them move into higher positions and will also teach them. When people teach, they can also learn. Kenzie makes sure that everyone at work knows how to do things. If someone tells her that they do not know how to do something, she teaches them.

I talked with someone else who is very special to me, Kris, about his experiences regarding business. Kris started his own business in high school selling home products out of a 53-foot semi-trailer in his backyard. He would purchase home products from online auctions by the pallet and resell them on other platforms like eBay and Facebook Marketplace. He got into Facebook

Marketplace early in its growth period, so he was able to capitalize on its early boom. He would review the products and make sure they were good enough to sell, and he would do what he needed to do to make them better. He sold things from shoe racks to cars. Before Kris had his own business, he was around his dad's construction business. Kris was exposed to entrepreneurship when he was 9 years old. Before he even said anything to clients, he heard what was going on. He learned how to be a conversationalist from being around small businesses for so long.

Something that Kris' friends would say about him is that he is a great conversationalist. He knows how to make people think through his words and he is also very kind, which makes it a great experience to talk with Kris. He told me how much he has been influenced by small business, and the main things he stressed were that he learned how to converse from business, and he learned about how to treat people. He learned how to notice negative reactions and learned to be cautious of what he says. He learned about saying what he meant from working in the construction business. In the book that I referenced in the first chapter, *The Four Agreements,* Ruiz wrote about saying what you mean, and this made up one of the four agreements. That agreement is to be impeccable with your word (Ruiz 34). [1]

Kris had many takeaways from being part of a small business for so long. He learned how to talk to people from his experiences with small businesses. He also learned what it was like to have a client no-show him, lie to him, and offer him far lower than he thought he earned. From doing business, one will experience undesired circumstances like the ones Kris experienced. Through business, Kris learned to treat people like plants.

He tends to combine his personal life with his work life. When he has good relationships with his coworkers, it is easier to do so. He believes that in business, one of the goals should be to never make enemies but to instead make friends. Kris's mantra is, "People will not forget how you made them feel." He lives by this in the way he treats people. I believe that Kris knows how to treat people like plants. He treats me like a plant. When I need less or more of something, he responds to it. He understands that we each have our own lives but that our lives are better with each other in them. Kris treats me with the respect and care that I want. I will never forget how he has made me feel.

Businesses can treat people like plants by aiming to make people happy. They can treat their customers and their employees like plants. They can show everyone involved that the business has great values and cares about all people. When a business treats people like plants, it adapts to the needs of the people. A business that treats people like plants notices when people need a different amount of water or sunlight. A manager can treat their employees like plants by noticing when they are starting to struggle. Businesses must remember, just like all people should, that you should not try to change a plant but instead change the environment in which it grows.

I talked to my mom about owning a business. She owned her own business when she was in her 20s. The advertising agency she was working for before opening her business went out of business. She had already been doing freelance work for about a year. It was a recession, and everyone at the ad agency lost their jobs. I asked her why she decided to open her business, and she told me that she asked herself, "Why not?" She started out doing freelancing and people started suggesting to her to have a real business. She also started getting lots of requests for projects. The business officially started in March of 1990, when she was 26 years old.

From it, she learned about treating people like plants. She learned that she needed to be able to pay her employees enough but that she also needed to support herself. She learned from owning her own business that you must customize certain discussions. It is important to see that different people need different things. Just like different plants need to be cared for in ways that vary from each other, people are different too and cannot be expected to need the same things. If you are a leader, you must focus on that. People should be treated how they individually want and need to be treated. Being a leader takes a lot of serious thought. You must do the best you can do. You also have limitations and you do not want to put yourself out of business.

I asked her what she learned about making her employees happy. She learned not to micromanage the employees that did not thrive with micromanagement. Leaders should do their best to customize their style towards each person as much as they can. She knows her current job well enough to be essentially left alone, and she loves that her manager recognizes and embraces that. Leaders can make their employees happy by making expectations as clear as possible. You should provide the best benefits you can afford for them. Make them feel special and vital. They are there to work, so they should work hard. They should be working hard enough to feel like they have contributed and they are appreciated, but do not burn them out. They need adequate time off. Money is important, but money is not everything. Employees want to feel safe, cared about, and appreciated.

My mom learned about treating herself like a plant when she decided to switch from owning her own graphic design business to going to nursing school and becoming a nurse. She decided that she was not happy owning her own business anymore and that she wanted to be an employee instead of having to tend to employees. She worked many hours as a business owner and says she was so busy working that she could not even enjoy her life. She is now a nursing webmaster, meaning that she is the head of creating and maintaining nursing websites. My mom's advice is that if you find yourself in a situation that is not healthy, mentally or physically, you are able to change it. You are not compelled to keep doing what you are doing simply because you set out to do it. Sometimes, change is necessary.

I asked my mom how she has been treated like a plant as an employee. She told me that she feels like she is being treated like a plant when she is treated with respect. She likes when others make her feel creative and wanted. She likes to feel like her ideas matter. In her current job, her manager puts her family first. If her family needs her, she can take time off work. Family is the most important thing in the world to my mother. In her current job, she has been able to mold her role throughout the past 10 years and she loves that about it. She also loves that she feels important where she works. She feels that many people rely on her. Feeling important, seen, and heard by others at work is vital.

I talked to my friend Ryan about training. Ryan believes that training is essential for businesses that want to treat their employees like plants, and who want to watch their employees grow. He thinks that training should combine the thoughts of the employees and the ideas of the company. Ryan has felt like his opinion has always mattered at his company and that is very important to him. He has felt like his ideas, thoughts, and opinions have mattered since day one. His company spent three months training him and by the time he was put into the real work, he thoroughly understood his role. The best way for a business to grow is if it focuses on the growth of its employees. Ryan believes that women can bring new ideas and a new perspective to a company. Overall, Ryan thinks that proper training matters and also thinks that different viewpoints can bring growth to businesses.

I dream of being an entrepreneur and owning my own business, and I am planning to have one that involves one of my favorite things in the world, which is coffee. I want my coffee shop to attract people who truly love coffee and who understand that coffee gives them so much more than just energy. Coffee, and the entire process that goes into making a cup, is so complex and interesting. Coffee comes from all over the world, and it tastes different based on its origin. Coffee has a story. We can share cups of coffee together. Coffee can connect us.

Not only do I love coffee, but I also love coffee shops. Coffee shops are places that can cultivate productivity, inspiration, and real human connections. I always have good and warm feelings when I walk into a coffee shop. The smells are magnificent. I love the hum of the espresso machine and the sound of chatter. In a coffee shop, you can be completely silent, or you can fully engage in a conversation. If you bring yourself something to do such as reading, writing, or working on your computer, you can appreciate the sounds around you, or you can wear headphones and enter your own world. Coffee shops are unlike anywhere else.

I asked Kris why he wants to own a business. He wants to own his own business because he likes solving problems. He told me that in a business you must address a passion and a problem. In the world, there are pyramid schemes and businesses that scam people, but there are also businesses that are trying to solve problems for the greater good. To have a great business, he will make sacrifices and put everything into it. He thinks that when you own a business, you start to become it because of the large time and emotional investment. To treat people like plants with his business, he hopes to watch them grow. If he does not see them grow, he wants to stop them from wilting. He understands that he might have to invest a different amount of time or energy into people if what he is doing is not working.

One of my mantras from the first chapter is to make this world a better place with your existence. This is about being what you want to see more of in this world, an idea that came from Gandhi. One thing I think the world needs more of is businesses that treat their employees like plants. Because of this, I want to own a business that treats people like plants. We need more businesses who pay employees livable or even great wages. We need more businesses that understand and cater to the needs of people. We need to become owners of businesses who do these things to make this world better for people.

Money is needed to make happiness in the workplace. To have a business, you need to have enough capital. In a business, you must make people happy. To make people happy using your business, you must have money. You have no choice. You can inspire your employees in ways other than monetary, but the baseline is monetary. Your employees need enough money to have a safe place to live and food to eat. You must pay them enough money to pay their bills.

I am interested in how HR and finance departments work together. I think if they work together well, they can make the company a much better place to work. HR sees people as assets whereas the finance department may see them as costs. The finance department sees a negative sign being associated with the people's wages and benefits, but the HR department sees additions to the workforce and possible additions of skills and traits that did not yet exist in the company. It is simply a different way of looking at it. Employees are not assets or expenses on the balance sheet, they are just seen as different to different departments. I see employees as assets, and I think they should be treated as such.

I think that businesses should practice what we all should practice, which is treating others with respect and kindness. We can all treat people like plants. We can understand that people want to feel needed, they want living or great wages, and they want to be heard. Money helps with having happier employees in a business. Business can teach us about communicating with people, and we must make sure that we keep in mind that people will remember how we made them feel. One of the main intentions of a business should be to make people happy.

LEFT BRAIN, RIGHT BRAIN, MY BRAIN

It is hard to imagine this world without art. It is also hard to imagine this world without math. Both art and math are essential for life as we know it. I had a long conversation with my friend, Maxime, about the importance of math and art and if one is more important than the other, and we agreed in the end that each could be very important depending on the taste and wants of different people. For example, one person may be a musician who is very interested in paintings. They also might travel mostly by foot, which eliminates the need for the engineering of a car for them. For this person, art is more important than math. For a person who works a job from Monday through Friday and uses their computer most of the time, math is likely more important than art in their life, unless their job is connected to art.

This brings me back to an idea that I mentioned in a previous chapter. If my book influences even one person, it was worth writing the entire thing. If what you do impacts even one person, it is valid and worth doing. Of course, we hope that what we do impacts more than just ourselves, but it does not really matter. We can remember to focus on bringing more goodness to this world, respecting ourselves and others, and treating people like plants.

Maybe you should bring goodness into this world by writing that book. You should finally start taking those photographs of flowers. You should start that business.

There are said to be two sides to our brains. The more left-brained people are thought to be more analytical and interested in math, whereas the more right-brained people are more creative and are interested in art. I have two very different sides to the things that interest me. I am interested in things that are associated with the right side of the brain like making coffee, cooking, baking, writing, creating, and music. I am also interested in things like math, finance, accounting, and science. I have always been interested in both sides, not just creative things and not just mathematical things.

I love math, but I also love art. I love art and I care deeply about aesthetics. My brain craves to be in an aesthetically pleasing environment. It is hard to be inspired in a place that does not make me feel something, but it is very easy to be inspired in a beautiful environment. Imagine how amazing you can feel in the forest, on the beach listening to the waves of the ocean, on the top of a mountain looking out at everything around you, at a cozy and tasteful coffee shop that plays some of your favorite songs on a record player, or in a yoga studio with the smells of incense and lavender and the flickering lighting of candles.

I am very influenced by math. I also love patterns. I have asked multiple people about why they love patterns, and these people are my friends who study majors such as computer science, engineering, and finance. They say they like the certainty of them and like the power to predict what is going to happen. One friend told me that a lot of life is unpredictable, so it feels good to be able to predict something about it.

I am not very good at assembling puzzles, but I think I am good at putting words together. I am also good with patterns. Writing a book is like putting together a puzzle. There are a whole bunch of words that you can choose from to arrange in a nice pattern that somehow has a logical beginning and end. At the end of a book, it becomes increasingly difficult to put together the words. On the other hand, a puzzle gets increasingly easier to put together when there are fewer spaces to fill with pieces. I like the way words can move people and the way they can make people feel so much.

Another thing I have learned because I am good at patterns and because I am good at memorization is Spanish. I started studying Spanish in 8th grade, and I have loved it since the start. I love the way it sounds coming off the tongue, and I love its romantic nature. I started learning Spanish using flashcards, and then I soon learned that I could simply write each vocabulary word down three times and then study it a few times and I would quickly learn all of the words. I studied Spanish for six years, and the next thing I want to do is live abroad to truly learn how to speak it well.

My friend, Morgan, thinks of herself as both left- and right-brained. She believes she is more mathematically brained and that her creativity comes from the patterns and formulas that she keeps on the math side. Like me, Morgan loves math and Spanish. She understands patterns, and they come easy to her. She loves math because her brain excels with it and because there is always an answer. She says it is like a game in her head and her brain just works that way. On the other hand, she loves art because it gives her a new perspective on life and makes her appreciate the world around her. She loves expressing herself by making art such as paintings. Like me, Morgan is both left- and right-brained.

I write more about this in the chapters regarding black and white thinking and lavender, but I think that there is something so beautiful about the unknown. Artists who put their art into the world show that they are fearless to opening up in a way and are willing to do things that are against the norm. Artists show others a glimpse inside of their minds. To be an artist, one must open their mind and be creative.

My friend explained to me that I spend a lot of time on the things and people that I like. I tend to invest a lot of energy into them. Some of the activities I really like that I spend a lot of time and energy on include making coffee, cooking, music, writing, getting to know people better, learning, and taking care of my mind and my body. I think that one of the reasons why this is the way my brain works is because I have an addictive personality. Because of it, I tend to find that I cannot get enough of some things if I really enjoy something about them. I think that it is a good thing to take your time with people, and I think this involves giving people second chances. I believe in second chances, and I believe in unconditional love.

I think that artists are often a lot smarter than they think they are. I think that artists are in tune with patterns, and because of that, they could potentially be very good at math. I also think that creativity disconnects people from society and can make them unsure of themselves when they receive negative reactions to their thoughts and work. Because they are rejected in a sense, they might feel like they are not good enough or what they are doing is not valid. They might also struggle to take interest in math because their brains are sometimes not oriented in that way. Creative people are very smart, and the things they create are worth creating if it brings happiness to even just them.

MATH

I love math. I believe in numbers. I like percentages, times, dates, and distances. I think math is all about patterns. Just as I believe that artists are often smarter than they think they are, simply because they understand patterns, I also believe that artists can be adept at math. I think of myself as someone good at both creative things and at math, and I think that many other people understand this great combination. When we can understand math and at the same time be creative, we have the power to create something incredible.

There is an idea that you should not be nice to people who are not nice to you. I believe that we should be nice to everyone, no matter what. I believe that we should treat others with kindness. When we put negative energy into negative energy, it simply puts more negative energy into the world. A negative and a negative does not equal a positive in this situation. This is not multiplication; it creates a negative. It is addition. It is math.

It is not hard to be nice. If we find it easy to be mean to people, we should give that some thought. It should be easy for us to be kind to people, and it helps if we always practice being kind to others, even to those who are unkind to us. It should be something that comes naturally, just as I believe that hate is something that we learn, and love is something that we all have.

I love the number seven. I have heard that there is something special about hearing or seeing something seven times and that this is the number where something becomes part of a person's memory. I like to make simple study guides whenever I want to learn something. If I look at it seven times, it usually is enough for me to be able to envision it in my mind. I believe there is magic in the number seven.

I believe that numbers do not lie, and that is why I love research. I love to read about studies that have been done and the statistics that have been found from them. I know that if something is popular, it means a lot or a high percentage of people like it. I know that many things in life are simply a numbers game. If we do something or try enough times, we might succeed. I also know that much of marketing and getting books out to the hands of readers is a game of numbers. If each person who reads a book recommends it to a few people, the word of mouth turns into the multiplication of readers. I believe in the word of mouth, and I believe in sharing things that we like with each other.

I think that math also exists in art because math is all about patterns. I wrote about how artists are often smarter than they think they are in the previous chapter. I think this is because artists can relate to, create, or know a lot about patterns. Musicians know which notes sound good together and which ones do not. Likewise, painters know the colors that look good together and the ones that do not. However, the difference between math and art is creativity. It is the link between the black and white and the middle of it all, which I call the art. In my eyes, art lies between the black and white.

To be able to write well, a person must understand math. Math shows itself in poetry, essays, articles, and books. Writing can be seen as an equation. The reader first must be introduced to the topics of the writing, and then the writer can go on to more complicated topics. In writing, ideas add onto already existing ideas to form something new. Letters in the alphabet have numbers that correspond to them. Words themselves are put together by letters, which are represented by numbers, which makes them mathematical. Putting words together logically and pleasantly requires skills with math. Being a conversationalist and a good communicator is mathematical.

Words fit together with grammatical rules. Sentences fit together with patterns, and patterns are mathematical. In the chapter about my brain, I wrote about how I am not very good at making puzzles, but I consider myself to be good at putting words together. I enjoy writing poetry, journaling, and I have thoroughly enjoyed writing this book. In a book, I think it gets harder to put words together after more words have been written. On the other hand, it becomes easier to put together a puzzle as more pieces have been placed. I like starting with a bigger picture. I like graphs, pictures, and numbers that make sense to me. Sometimes, numbers must be averaged or added together to make more sense in the context. Sometimes, you must make a graph or a simple table. Numbers can be numbers that do not make sense, just as letter orders, large spreadsheets of numbers, and puzzles can be confusing. I am not very good at spelling in English. It is interesting because I am quite good at spelling in Spanish. I believe it is because I learned English from hearing it and not seeing it, and I learned Spanish using flashcards. The words became engraved in my mind. I am a very analytical person. I am also a very visual person.

A definition of creativity is that it is, "The tendency to generate or recognize ideas, alternatives, or possibilities that may be useful in solving problems, communicating with others, and entertaining ourselves and others." [25] I think that creative people can often bring words to a conversation that a person who is not creative would not. In general, I believe that creative people are often better conversationalists.

As the definition states, creativity not only helps with communicating with others, but it is also useful in solving problems. Because of this, I think that the most successful entrepreneurs are creative, and because creativity can lead to better communication and problem solving, great entrepreneurs know how to do both of these skills and they also know how to handle money. Indeed, a well-known job site, lists creativity as the number one characteristic of a successful entrepreneur. The other characteristics included passion, motivation, the ability to network, optimism, and self-confidence. [26]

The article about the characteristics of a successful entrepreneur lists some ideas for each characteristic. For creativity, the site recommends developing habits that support the creative system. It says to do this by dedicating a part of your day to things that make you feel inspired and creative, and suggests that these things might be music, meeting new people, or reading. It recommends doing this thing in the dedicated part of your day and to let your mind flow. The second characteristic, passion, can be enhanced by focusing on why you are doing your work and the meaning it has to you, focusing on your objective, and helping others. Another characteristic is the ability to connect with people, and it helps entrepreneurs gain knowledge and promote their goods or services. [26] Great entrepreneurs approach others intending to have a real human connection.

Going back to the idea that creative people can have more interesting conversations, we tend to associate with people who are of a similar intellectual level to us. To form a deep connection, people desire to feel intellectually compatible. It is easier to have conversations with those that think similarly to how we do, and with people who are as clever, or maybe more clever, than we are. Intelligent people tend to associate with other intelligent people. We seek those who are compatible with us. If we like and understand math, we might associate with others who are similar. Analytical people seek out other analytical people. Creative people find those who are also creative. Sometimes, people are both. Those who are both will associate with both. We should strive to also associate with those that are different than us.

We have friends and people that we know, and we also have people that we truly know. The difference in the ones that we truly know is that we have spent hours talking to and learning about them. We can learn so much from the people we meet and the people we know. We can learn even more from the people we truly know. They teach us things, they tell us stories, and they help us grow. The people who we love and form friendships with are the people who change us, teach us, influence us, and make this life so beautiful. As I have written before, you are the only one you will spend the entirety of your life with. You are alone in a sense, but at the same time you are not alone because there are millions of other humans on this earth. People are fascinating because they are art. They tell stories, and these stories are art, too.

Money, in addition to creativity, ties into the title of this chapter, Math. I think that money in business is essential for keeping people happy. I believe in non-profit businesses, or at least ones that are for the greater good. Businesses changed so much in 2020, and the pandemic explains it. Companies have been taking shortcuts because it is easier and cheaper. It has always interested me to use business, something that can so easily be cutthroat, as something that helps people. I have known for a long time that I want to help people.

I learned about calculations related to money from swimming. A place where I learned a lot about math was the pool. In swimming, a person must care about times and split times and know how they are progressing to get faster. In swimming, numbers are very important. One-hundredth of a second can mean the difference between making the cut for a meet or winning a race. I learned about doing math from the time intervals for sets and from calculating the lengths in each swim based on the number of yards. I learned about money by comparing a quarter to 25 yards, or the length of most pools I swim in. Swimming taught me about numbers and math.

I think money buys happiness in business. I know from studying finance and all the other components of business that money is essential for success. Money is essential in business to keep the employees happy and well paid, and it is essential to keep the business running smoothly. It is also essential because if there is extra money there can be an emergency fund in case of something terrible happening like the effects of the coronavirus on many small businesses. However, what buys happiness in life is not money, but instead, it is relationships. Studies have shown numerous times that satisfying and reliable relationships are linked to happiness and better health. Our relationships cause our strongest emotions. Positive relationships are beautiful and powerful, and they can lead to us having all-around better lives.

Even though I think that money buys happiness in business, I also think that businesses must do more than just paying their employees enough. They must listen to what the employees want and need and what they are saying about their leaders. In order to be successful, a company must have solid HR management, never be too focused on profit, always focus on happiness, and treat people how they want to be treated. A goal of life, and in my opinion, business relationships too, is to treat everyone and yourself like a plant.

Something that can lead to having a more comfortable life is having enough money to cover basic needs. A person must understand how much money they make to understand how much money they can spend. Some basic needs that are bought with money are putting roofs over our heads, food on our tables, and clothes on our bodies. By understanding math, inflows, and outflows, it is easier to allocate one's money to the necessary places instead of to unnecessary spending.

I believe that I have the power to be an entrepreneur. To start a business, one must understand patterns and math. They also must understand that a business needs money to thrive. My mom was an entrepreneur. Her business was designing logos, brochures, corporate stationery, flyers, mailers, and direct marketing pieces. My mother has many mantras, but when I asked her the main one that she used in her business she said, "Form follows function follows form," because to her, the functionality of something is very important, but the way something looks is also very important. A design concept, and more specifically a 19th century architecture and design construct, is that form follows function, which means that the way something looks and or the shape of a building should primarily relate to its function.

She believes that the form, or the way something looks, is in many ways more important than the function, or the way it works. She says that sometimes, people judge books by their cover because you would not think to pick up a book with an unattractive cover unless someone recommended it to you. She told me that the book must match its cover, while also drawing people in. The form is the first most important part of design.

She mostly did work for medical companies. She was interested in doing that because she liked the premise of healthcare and directly impacting people's lives for the better. She liked the selflessness of it. Because of this, after the 17th year of owning her own graphic design business, she decided she wanted to go back to school. She decided to become a nurse. She did an intense and fast-paced nursing program and graduated from nursing school while raising her children. She worked with patients for three years, and then after realizing that she wanted to utilize her other skill set that was being left unused and that she was tired of missing her kids' events because of working weekends, late nights, and night shifts, she applied for a different job. She wanted to blend her skill sets. She applied to be the webmaster of nursing websites, and she got the job. She had to learn a lot about the web and take a few classes, but she has always enjoyed learning.

Something I learned from my mom is to directly impact others instead of simply appealing to someone's taste. You know deep down what makes you special and what simply feels right. You know your passions, and you should pursue them. I learned that from my mom. She wanted to use her brain more because she has a full spectrum of ways to apply her creativity and knowledge, and she also loves math. Math is incredibly important in design. Your brochure must fold correctly and in nursing, you must give the right amount of medication. To do these things, she had to understand math.

Math makes me think of numbers, percentages, popularity, science, the word of mouth, and distances. It makes me think of multiplication, division, addition, and subtraction. It makes me think of calculus and thinking of all these things makes me happy. It reminds me of solving problems and getting to a solution that is exactly what I want to see. It makes me think of the security that I feel when I know something has been researched and proven by science and experimentation. I love math, and math has taught me so much.

THE ISSUES WITH BLACK AND WHITE THINKING

There is an indescribable amount of black and white thinking in the world. It is almost like people forget that there is a middle ground to an infinite number of questions. Black and white thinking is like putting people in a box. It is the disillusioned idea that knowing one thing about someone can tell you everything about them. People act like there are only two types of people: good and bad. People act like there are only two political parties. People act like there are only a few religions that exist. People act like their way is the right way, and that the way others do something is wrong. People act like there is a predetermined right from wrong, and they do not like themselves when they do not live up to their idea of the "right thing to do." People act like there is only one way to do something, and that is "the right way." People also act as if they can only associate with people who are like them. This type of thinking is black and white thinking, and it tears us apart.

Division of people is often not good. We can all try to live more harmoniously and peacefully with others. A leap towards this is genuinely being kind to everyone you meet. A fact of life is that people tend to gossip about each other, and they tend to be mean to each other. Kids do it, and adults do it too. People gossip because others are different from them, and they gossip when others do things they think are “wrong”. The world could also be a better place if we all just understood that we are all human beings, and we are all imperfect. We are here to live our lives, not to judge the lives of others. It is so unnecessary to spend the time we have on this earth judging and being mean to others.

Something we must start to understand more collectively is that political views and parties are often based highly on economic opinions and opinions about the fundamentals of government. Much of it is based on whether you think the government should be involved more or less than it currently is. Because we do not have a prominent third party in the U.S., many people do not even realize that there could be another party that they might fit into. However, instead of having three large parties, the U.S. is divided. Because the U.S. is almost exactly split down the middle of Democrats and Republicans, some people decide that they will only associate with those of their party and will not even take a moment to ask themselves the most important questions of all. Does this person dislike and judge others based on what they cannot control? Are they sexist, racist, or homophobic? Are they kind or cruel to others or me?

I did not think about these questions before moving to Missouri for college in 2017. When I started to learn more about the quaint town of St. Charles, Missouri, I found that the majority of its people are Republicans. Where I grew up, on the other hand, there was a mix of political views. In St. Charles,

I was introduced a few times as, "This is my liberal friend." Someone once said, "You're actually a liberal?" I quickly realized that so many of the people around me were of a different political party than I was. I also realized that they were not evil for having different views than me, and that many of those with different views than me were often actually very nice and respectful people. It makes me think that if we are friends only with people who agree with our political views, we would then only allow half of the U.S. population to be our friends, even if they could be our greatest friends.

We can be friends with people of opposite political parties than us. It is absurd to me that we even divide ourselves by political parties, but it makes sense because it is a black and white approach, and people fall into black and white thinking so easily. We can find similarities with almost anyone. We can talk about so much more than politics and things that make us disagree. We can talk about our lives, food, music, our travels, our families, and our friends. If, during a friendship, we find that someone has differing views from us, we need to consider if these views are rooted in the hate for others based on an uncontrollable variable, or if it is based on economics and the government.

People often think in black and white when they think about people. They think about skin, sexual orientation, gender, and economic status. We are all individuals, and we are all different. I believe that we are all uniquely ourselves. We are all stars in a galaxy together, shining bright. We can find the light inside of each other, regardless of who we are, where we come from, and what we look like. We were meant to live harmoniously on this planet together.

Many instances in 2020 had to do with black and white thinking. When everything happened after George Floyd's passing, many people decided that all police offers are bad people. This is an instance of black and white thinking. Because some police are "bad", it does not mean that they all are. Because some police are racists, it does not mean that they all are. I do not think that we should abolish the police, but I do think that we need reform and change. We need more educated police who know about psychology. We also could send more than police and paramedics to psychiatric emergencies. We could send therapists and people trained in psychology to go to the scene, too. It cannot be so black and white.

I have many friends who belong to different political parties than me and have many different beliefs. I am close with some people who are genuinely very different than me. One of those people is my friend, JeAnnah. JeAnnah and I have been friends since before I can remember since our brothers became friends when they were about 10 years old. JeAnnah and I disagree on so many things that it might seem unbelievable to an outsider that we get along so well. JeAnnah has taught me so much about lavender friendships. She has taught me how to have a civil disagreement about something and to be able to move past it. Even though we have differing views, we both understand that we have good intentions as people. In many disagreements, there is a common ground between the sides. I love finding the common ground. I love to find the lavender. It is also beautiful to realize that despite all the differences you and someone have, you have similarities too. You have things you can talk about no matter what, simply because you are human. We are all different, but we are equal.

My dad and I are also very different people. We have always been different, but we love each other and there is lavender between us. He says that one of our differences is the way we look at things. I see the world with lots of wonder and awe, but he looks at life with a troubleshooting mentality. He is always trying to make everything better. Even as a little kid, he liked to take things apart and put them back together. He has always liked to fix things. I do not have much interest in fixing material objects or troubleshooting them. I like big ideas and thinking about fixing issues between people. I think about black and white and how we can learn to accept people as they are without trying to change or "fix" them but to instead find lavender.

We look at the world differently, but we also have similarities. One of those similarities is that once we put our minds to something or accept a challenge, we strive to do it. We are persistent people. My dad told me that he thinks that I am creative because of my mom, but I think that he also is creative. He writes code and does computer programming, and there are many ways to be creative in this. My mom explained that my dad and I are both capable of making quick decisions, we both care about helping people, and we are both detail-oriented. She also said that my dad strives to stay neutral. He finds lavender between himself and others, especially when it comes to family. Some people find it much too difficult to be kind to those with different opinions. I think that a similarity I share with my dad is caring about people. We both pay attention to the little details of what people want and like, and I think I learned about doing that from him.

I talked with my dad about his mantras. One of his mantras is to be proactive. He does not think it is good to procrastinate. Starting tasks sooner rather than later helps with the anxiety and stress that comes with them, and it also allows the time needed to do a job well done. Another one of his mantras is to learn something from everyone. This mantra relates to the idea of black and white thinking because we can learn from those who are different than us. If people have different opinions, they may find it easier to avoid each other and the conversations between each other. Having conversations with people who are different than us can allow us to find lavender areas. We can learn to understand that different is not bad.

Another person I have many differences with is my friend, Paul. I have known Paul since elementary school, but we were not friends until high school. He says we are different in superficial ways. We have different political views and many different views in general. We have always talked about how it is strange that we can get along so well and have such differing opinions and views. However, he is one of my favorite people. Some of the ways that Paul and I are similar is that we value family, education, and respect. Paul and I had similar upbringings and went to the same elementary, middle, and high schools.

One of Paul's mantras is that "It's nice to be important, but it's more important to be nice", which is a quote from The Rock. Paul says it is important to treat people equally. He believes in treating people and yourself with respect. He thinks we should always do our best, and that we should be honest to ourselves and others. I am so thankful that Paul and I saw past our differences and were able to become such great friends. I feel lucky to have his friendship.

My other friend that is very different than me is Ryan. We have different political views, but we can find so many other similarities between us. We also can find similarities in our political views. Ryan is from Missouri. Ryan played baseball and basketball, and I had never really talked to people who played those sports before I met him. Ryan reminded me of my dad. They are both straight to the point, and they think linearly. They like to have back-up plans, and change can be difficult for them until they adapt to it. The most beautiful similarity is that they will do anything for the people they love.

When I talked to Ryan, he told me that he believes the world is not black and white. Social issues and people are not black and white. You cannot put everything in just two places. When people think too much in black and white, it produces hatred towards the other thinking or side. If you do not agree with others, they should still be able to tell you how they feel. We should be able to understand each other's views. People get so wrapped up in one viewpoint that they cannot even begin to understand where someone else is coming from. Black and white thinking generates stereotypes for specific groups. People do not fit into only one side. We are all different.

Today, two people with disagreeing views often struggle to have a rational conversation. If Ryan and I had thought we could not be friends because of differing political views, we would have missed out on a great friendship. Politics are highly based on social issues currently but what also drives people to be a certain party is economics. Through my many conversations with Ryan over the years, I have learned that we have so many agreements despite our disagreements. I would have never known how similar we were if I would have decided not to be friends with someone who seemed so different than me.

The reason that Ryan belongs in this chapter about the issue with black and white thinking is that there is a high chance that I would never have talked to him before going to school in Missouri. Ryan initiated the conversation for the first time. I was unsure about it, but because my friend Grant told me that Ryan was a nice guy, I decided I would talk to him. Ryan and I have talked regularly since our freshman year of college. He is one of my best friends. We were able to have very interesting conversations about many different topics, including topics that I have never discussed with anyone else. It is quite amazing when you find someone who understands you intellectually.

We need to think about black and white, and we need to consider if we see things as black and white. We should associate ourselves with people who are different than us, even if this means following people who are different than us on social media. We need to make sure we are not putting people in groups in our heads because we are all different anyway. Once again, we are different, but we are equal. Once we can see past our differences, we will find lavender.

LAVENDER

Between black and white is color. One of those colors is lavender. Lavender is a color that is similar to grey. It is also more earthy and feminine of a color than grey. Lavender in Spanish is "la lavanda," a word with a feminine pronoun, just like the moon, the stars, women, and the Earth. Lavender to me symbolizes grey areas. The bottom of a rainbow is purple. Just like purple, I belong near and close to the Earth. When I feel closer to the Earth, I also feel closer to the other living beings on it. I love grey areas, and I love to think between black and white. I hope to make you realize the connection between things, especially between the stars, the sun and the moon, the trees, masculinity and femininity, and between all of us.

There is a more lavender way of thinking than to think in only black and white. This is a lighter and more blended approach than thinking about only grey areas. It is thinking about the lavender areas. These areas are things that often blend two different ideas or answers into one collectively "right" answer. It is the middle ground; it is the area that people do not always think about. Lavender is a light purple, it is not overpowering, and it is not seen in everything. Lavender flowers are a gift, just as the trees and all other plants are. Lavender happens when we see the light in others regardless of their differences.

Feelings and opinions change. As they change, they shift from one side to the other, and they might do so slowly, stopping for a while in between. Feelings and opinions might never be all to one side or the other, and that would make them lavender. To be lavender means something is in the middle, or it is changing. In the process of changing, one experiences lavender. Lavender is the steps and everything in between black and white, and between one side and another.

Lavender things are open to interpretation. Things that are lavender do not necessarily have rules, they are open to anything. Lavender often involves uncertainty and the area between mixed characteristics. To change, we must adopt new ideas and new ways. In doing this, we will experience the lavender in the middle. We cannot grow unless we change.

Imagine if we all worked like the trees. As I explained in a previous chapter, some trees work together, photosynthesizing and equally using nutrients, to ensure a healthy environment for other trees nearby. Some trees work harmoniously, just as people can. The U.S. is very individualistic and capitalistic, and it does not need to be this way. Other countries have found ways to make things work with a less individualistic approach, and many do it well. We need to work together to become happier.

I have written about the fact that I am a perfectionist. I love doing things very well, and I sometimes do not even see the point in doing them if it is not done greatly. I have found that in almost everything, there is room for error. For example, if you write an essay or take a test and get a 90% on it, you probably got the same letter grade as someone who got a 100%. However, you did not have to stress yourself out as much as that other person. You made small errors and you were okay with it because you knew it was not worth that extra amount of stress. You knew you would do alright. That 10% of whatever you did not get those points for could have been an extra touch you added that your professor just did not like. It might have even seemed artistically good to you. This shows that there might be art that lies in that 10% of mistakes. The 10% might be the fun part. I see that 10% as lavender.

I see something significant about our '20s. I see something special about the 2020s, and I think there was something unique about the 1920s as well. I think that the '20s are a time for messing up a little bit. They are a time for living, for figuring out who we are. 2020 for me was a year of growth. I think a lot of people grew that year and learned about themselves. I think that these next years will be for recovery and growth, and I hope that we continue to learn. I hope we continue to make changes and that we see the lavender in between everything. I also think about the fact that a human could have about 100 years in their life. I think that when you do many things, you can do them 90% great and then leave the last 10% to do however you want to do it, and I think that your life can be like that, too. I think that a person's 20s can be used for experimentation. We get to have fun with 10% of all of this, and I think that art lies in the 10%.

Lavender understands that perfection is not something we should strive for. Lavender knows that there is something between imperfect and perfect in terms of looks, and something between those two is beautiful. Your arms, your legs, your stomach, and your face are all beautiful. They all show who you are, and they do it wonderfully. You were made with such delicacy and care, and it shows. Your body loves you and it is ready for you to love it back.

In lavender areas, it is difficult to see what is right and what is wrong. This is because the whole concept of right and wrong is an idea of black and white thinking. Right and wrong are ideas based on what has been planted inside of us since the day we were born. Right and wrong are what we have learned from our parents, our siblings, our teachers, and our friends. Right and wrong do not actually exist, we just made it up. In lavender areas, we do not think about what is right and what is wrong. We simply see everything as it is, without putting sides to it. Life is not in black and white; we see it in millions of different colors. Things are between one thing and another.

In life, we learn about right and wrong. However, we are not taught that gay is wrong unless we are taught out of hate, and we are not taught that darker colored skins are wrong or lesser than light ones unless we are taught with hate. We learn right and wrong when we learn that showing people kindness and love is the right thing to do, and when our parents show us kindness, generosity, and compassion, we learn how to do things the way they do. We learn from our parents because if they show us love and show us what we want to see, we want to do what they do. They are important to us, and we learn from them.

We should try to live in the lavender areas. We should have lavender thoughts and in doing so we can treat people like plants. We can realize that all plants are similar in a way because they all need water and sunlight, just like we as humans need other people and we need to feel loved and cared about. As people, love and care are our sunlight and water. These things are absolutely essential. By living in the lavender areas, we realize that we all have differences but are all connected. Some of the things that remind me of lavender are being open-minded, forward-thinking, adaptive, and communicative. I think of change, progress, unity, peace, diversity, and togetherness.

Seeing everything in black and white creates division. In this world, we need more unity. We need more unity between countries, political parties, between people with different skin colors, the rich and the poor, the young and the old, between genders, and between any person who is different from another person, which is every person. We need to treat people like plants. We need to strive to create good in this world with our existence. We need to grow for the rest of our lives. We need to spread light and love. We must remember that we are all different, but we are equal. We do not need more black and white; we need more lavender.

WORKS CITED

1. Ruiz, Don Miguel. *The Four Agreements*. Amber-Allen Publishing, 1997.
2. Thomée, Sara et al. "Mobile Phone Use and Stress, Sleep Disturbances, and Symptoms of Depression among Young Adults--a Prospective Cohort Study." *BMC public health,* U.S. National Library of Medicine, 31 Jan. 2011, https://pubmed.ncbi.nlm.nih.gov/21281471/. Accessed 21 June 2021.
3. Mark, Emily. "Taoism." *Ancient History Encyclopedia,* Ancient History Encyclopedia, 22 February 2016, www.ancient.eu/Taoism/. Accessed 21 March 2021.
4. Rahula, Walpola Sri. "The Noble Eightfold Path: Meaning and Practice." *Tricycle,* 28 May 2019, tricycle.org/magazine/noble-eightfold-path/. Accessed 21 March 2021.
5. Mark, Joshua J. "The Mayan Pantheon: The Many Gods of the Maya." *Ancient History Encyclopedia*, Ancient History Encyclopedia, 7 July 2012, www.ancient.eu/article/415/the-

mayan-pantheon-the-many-gods-of-the-maya/.
Accessed 21 March 2021.

6. History.com Editors. "Teotihuacan." *History.com*, A&E Television Networks, 21 Aug. 2018, www.history.com/topics/ancient-americas/teotihuacan. Accessed 21 March 2021.
7. Rosenthal, Sheri. *Teotihuacán: A Spiritual Mystery School,* Date not found, journeysofthespirit.com/teotihuacan-a-spiritual-mystery-school/. Accessed 25 February 2021.
8. "Gender Identity & Roles: Feminine Traits & Stereotypes." *Planned Parenthood,* Date not found, www.plannedparenthood.org/learn/gender-identity/sex-gender-identity/what-are-gender-roles-and-stereotypes. Accessed 2 March 2021.
9. "Suicide Statistics." *American Foundation for Suicide Prevention*, American Foundation for Suicide Prevention, Mar. 2021, afsp.org/suicide-statistics/. Accessed 13 Jan 2021.
10. Population Reference Bureau. "Around the Globe, Women Outlive Men." *PRB,* 1 Sept. 2001, www.prb.org/resources/around-the-globe-women-outlive-men/. Accessed 13 Jan. 2021.

11. Waldron, I, and S Johnston. "Why do women live longer than men?" *Journal of human stress*, U.S. National Library of Medicine, June 1976, https://pubmed.ncbi.nlm.nih.gov/1018115/. Accessed 13 Jan. 2021.

12. Woolley, Anita, and Thomas W Malone. "Defend Your Research: What Makes a Team Smarter? More Women." *Harvard Business Review*, June 2011, hbr.org/2011/06/defend-your-research-what-makes-a-team-smarter-more-women. Accessed 26 Jan. 2021.

13. Arenal, Concepción. "La Mujer Del Porvenir: Capítulo 8. ¿Qué Oficios y Profesiones Pueden Ejercer Las Mujeres?" *"Capítulo 8. ¿Qué Oficios y Profesiones Pueden Ejercer Las Mujeres?" in "La Mujer Del Porvenir" on Manifold Scholarship at CUNY*, Date not found, cuny.manifoldapp.org/read/la-mujer-del-porvenir/section/b5a4a160-6d62-4f21-a4e5-024ee931a590. Accessed 29 March 2021.

14. Goleman, Dan. "Are Women More Emotionally Intelligent Than Men?" *Psychology Today*, Sussex Publishers, 29 Apr. 2011, www.psychologytoday.com/us/blog/the-brain-and-emotional-intelligence/201104/are-women-more-emotionally-intelligent-men. Accessed 29 March 2021.

15. Chaplin, Tara M. "Gender and Emotion Expression: A Developmental Contextual Perspective." *Emotion Review : Journal of the International Society for Research on Emotion*, U.S. National Library of Medicine, 16 June 2016, www.ncbi.nlm.nih.gov/pmc/articles/PMC4469291/. Accessed 29 March 2021.

16. Browning, Frank. "Survival Secrets: What Is It About Women That Makes Them More Resilient Than Men?" *Cal Alumni Association*, 29 Apr. 2015, alumni.berkeley.edu/california-magazine/just-in/2015-04-30/survival-secrets-what-it-about-women-makes-them-more. Accessed 29 March 2021.

17. Ortiz-Ospina, Esteban, and Diana Beltekian. "Why Do Women Live Longer than Men?" *Our World in Data*, 14 Aug. 2018, ourworldindata.org/why-do-women-live-longer-than-men. Accessed 10 April 2021.

18. Mindworks Team. "What Are the Different Types of Meditation? Benefits (With Examples)." *Mindworks Meditation*, Date not found, mindworks.org/blog/different-types-meditation-technique/. Accessed 10 June 2021.

19. Smith, Jeremy Adam, et al. "10 Things We Know About the Science of Meditation." *Mindful*, 12 Nov. 2018, www.mindful.org/10-things-we-know-about-the-science-of-meditation/. Accessed 20 February 2021.

20. Chamorro-Premuzic, Tomas, and Cindy Gallop. "7 Leadership Lessons Men Can Learn from Women." *Harvard Business Review*, 1 Apr. 2020, hbr.org/2020/04/7-leadership-lessons-men-can-learn-from-women. Accessed 22 March 2021.

21. "Men or Women: Who's the Better Leader?" *Pew Research Center's Social & Demographic Trends Project*, Pew Research Center, 25 Aug. 2008, www.pewresearch.org/social-trends/2008/08/25/men-or-women-whos-the-better-leader/. Accessed 22 March 2021.

22. Rudow, Heather. "Strength in Numbers: Women Are More Optimistic than Men Because of Their Close Friendships." *Counseling Today*, 4 Oct. 2011, ct.counseling.org/2011/10/strength-in-numbers-women-are-more-optimistic-than-men-because-of-their-close-friendships/. Accessed 22 March 2021.

23. Eckel, Catherine C., and Philip J. Grossman. "Are Women Less Selfish Than Men?: Evidence from Dictator Experiments." *The Economic Journal*, vol. 108, no. 448, pp. 726–735. *JSTOR*, 1998, www.jstor.org/stable/2565789. Accessed 28 March 2021.

24. Delmore, Erin. "This Is How Women Voters Decided the 2020 Election." *NBCNews.com*, NBCUniversal News Group, 13 Nov. 2020, www.nbcnews.com/know-your-value/feature/how-women-voters-decided-2020-election-ncna1247746. Accessed 28 March 2021.

25. Franken, Robert E, and Robert W W Weisberg. *What Is Creativity?*, Date not found, www.csun.edu/~vcpsy00h/creativity/define.htm. Accessed 1 May 2021.

26. "15 Entrepreneur Characteristics To Develop." *Indeed Career Guide*, 1 Apr. 2021, www.indeed.com/career-advice/finding-a-job/entrepreneur-characteristics. Accessed 1 May 2021.

Made in the USA
Columbia, SC
11 November 2021